When JESUS Speaks to a GRIEVING HEART

Janice Thompson

BARBOUR BOOKS
An Imprint of Barbour Publishing, Inc.

INTRODUCTION

. . . .

This intimate devotional—written for those who are grieving—will bring comfort in times of loss. Whether you're facing the loss of a loved one, a job, or a dream, there's something in this little book for you. Dozens of readings offer the comfort, encouragement, and hope you need to face the day, along with lovely little reminders that Jesus has a very personal message to help you through this difficult season.

You will learn that Jesus speaks every day—in every difficult situation—to bring comfort, grace, healing, and hope. Each devotional, rooted in scripture and written from Christ's heavenly perspective, will leave you feeling encouraged to pick up the pieces and to move forward with His hand in yours.

"Blessed are those who mourn,
for they will be comforted."
MATTHEW 5:4 NIV

Consumed

This is my comfort in my affliction,
for Your word has given me life.

PSALM 119:50 NKJV

You feel consumed by grief. Your heart is broken in half, and you wonder if it will ever be pieced back together. Oh, how I long to heal those broken places! Cling fast to My Word. It will not fail you. Within its pages I've made a promise that you will not be overtaken. My love for you is that strong. . .as it is for all My children. Days of suffering will come, yes. This is a broken world, after all. But I'm on your side. Look around you, My child. So many people need you. So many hands reach up to you. So many hearts cry out to you. How can I use you to minister to those who need you if you're consumed? I will help you dry those tears and gaze into the eyes of the people in your life who still (very much) need and want you with them. If you're open to it, I will guide you to counselors or mentors who can help you heal so that you're ready when the time comes. They will pour into you and aid in the healing I have in store. I will turn this for good, though it seems impossible at the moment. I love you too much to let this season of grief consume you. My hand is outstretched. Grab it and hold on tight. Don't let go, no matter how broken you feel on the inside. I love you.

Loss of a Friendship

. . . .

*And we know that in all things God works for
the good of those who love him, who have been
called according to his purpose.*

Romans 8:28 NIV

Friendship is one of My special gifts to you, My child. I've
surrounded you with wonderful people who link arms with
you and "do life" with you, through thick and thin. They
are My special gift to you, a family of sorts. Unfortunately,
I've witnessed broken friendships time and time again. It
breaks My heart to see you wounded by the very people
I've sent to care for you. This was never part of My plan.
I'm all about unity. Division can be devastating. I've seen
how these shake-ups affect you. You're hurt by the ones
who lash out, but you refuse to give up on your friends.
Your heart is filled with gratitude, even in the midst of
pain. And though you've felt the sting of betrayal at times,
you always brush yourself off and keep going. (I love that
about you!) I want you to know that I'm always here for
you, even when you're grieving the loss of a friend. I won't
leave you. I'll stick closer than a brother, no matter what.
Even if you get mad at Me, I'll be your very best friend.
Even if you're ready to turn and walk away, I won't. I'll
stick close. We'll be BFFs, no matter what.

Loss of a Marriage

One flesh. Torn. Ripped. Bleeding. You're wondering if you'll ever feel complete again. You don't know where to begin. How do you put the broken pieces back together? How will your heart ever heal? Oh, sweet child, I need you to know that this brokenness, this pain, will ease over time. My heart is just as shredded as yours. What has happened isn't My best for you. In fact, it's the opposite of what I had planned for you. This was never meant to happen. But you and Me? . . . We're okay. We're better than okay, actually. I'll hold your hand. I'll be the One you share your deepest secrets with, and I'll never betray you. Never. Ever. So put your hand in Mine. Let's renew our vows to one another, shall we? I'll never leave you. I'll never forsake you. That's a commitment you will never have to question, from now until we meet face-to-face. I give you My assurance that better days are ahead. Keep your hand in Mine. This difficult season will soon be behind you. Your broken heart will heal. I promise.

COVERED AND CRADLED

. . . .

And he took the children in his arms,
placed his hands on them and blessed them.

MARK 10:16 NIV

My hands will cover you when you need shelter from the
storms of life. And they lift you, cradle you, when the grief
is overwhelming. Please don't ever doubt My love, no
matter the agony you're feeling on the inside. My love is
constant, never ending. It's the only thing you can count
on when everything else is crumbling. You might not
recognize the many ways I'm pouring out My affection
during this difficult season, but I'm right here. I'm not
going anywhere, I promise. And though you feel like you're
at the bottom of a well right now, I'm here, holding you,
just as I held the children in My arms to bless them in
days of old. Can you picture what that must have been
like, when I gathered the little ones into My arms to bless
them? Picture Me doing that very thing for you, sweeping
you into My loving arms to bring comfort, blessing, and
healing. You're not abandoned. There's light above. Look
up. My steadfast love will lift you from this place, and you
will be whole again. My arms are strong enough to hold
you, and I promise to never let go.

Through the Filter of Faith

. . . .

*Be gracious to me, O LORD, for
I am pining away; heal me, O LORD,
for my bones are dismayed.*

PSALM 6:2 NASB

I hear your questions. You're trying to process what's happening through the filter of your faith. You've begun to doubt My love, My care. You're hearing from others how strong you are, but you don't feel strong. You've never felt weaker. This isn't how you planned it. This isn't how you thought it would be. You're struggling to understand the role your faith has played—or not played—in this difficult situation you're wading through. I want you to know that I can handle the hard questions. I also need you to hear My heart when I say that you don't have to go on trying to be strong. In fact, My work will be perfected in you when you admit your weakness and run to Me. You can't handle what's happened. Not on your own. But there's good news: I can. I can handle it all. Please allow Me to be the strong one. And while we're at it, let Me redefine your definition of trust. You might not always get the outcome you want, but I work every situation to My glory. Please don't give up. Don't stop trusting. Keep those heart-cries coming My way. I promise to answer, My child.

ABANDONMENT

"*Be strong and courageous, do not be afraid or tremble at them, for the LORD your God is the one who goes with you. He will not fail you or forsake you.*"

DEUTERONOMY 31:6 NASB

Someone you love has made the decision to leave, to walk out the door and not come back. It makes no sense. People are supposed to stay. They're supposed to take the word *commitment* seriously. And yet, here you are in an empty hallway, with the backside of the door staring you in the face, and you're wondering what you did to deserve it. Was it something you said? Something you should've done but didn't? Why have you been abandoned, left to fend for yourself? Were you not good enough? Loving enough? Beautiful enough? It's time to stop with the questions, My child. This isn't your doing. I will use this experience to deepen your understanding of devotion, if you will let Me. I will grow you into the kind of person who doesn't hurt others as you've been hurt. You will get past these feelings of abandonment. That gaping hole in your chest will soon be filled with My salve, My ointment. You'll experience love as you've never known before. . .if you just give that broken heart to Me. I will bolster your courage when you need it most. I will show you how to be strong. . .in time. For now, just draw near to Me and let the healing begin.

Death of a Child

....

*And I heard a voice from heaven, saying,
"Write, 'Blessed are the dead who die in the
Lord from now on!' " "Yes," says the Spirit,
"so that they may rest from their labors,
for their deeds follow with them."*

REVELATION 14:13 NASB

Disbelief. Shock. Guilt. You wonder if you're in a dream, a nightmare. You pray you'll wake up, and yet the horror goes on. Your arms are empty. Your heart is broken. You want to curl up in a ball and never wake up again. If only this nightmare would end. You're wondering how—or if—you will ever recover from the loss of your child. You want to believe that things will get better, but you need My help. I hear the questions, too painful to be uttered aloud: *Am I to blame? Did I cause this? What could I have done differently?* You have no closure. You wander aimlessly, your arms feeling empty, your heart barren. Oh, My sweet one, how I care about where you are and what you've lost. Please don't let your heart grow numb for long. I will bring healing, I promise. I will apply ointment to that shattered heart. It's impossible to believe right now, I know, but there will truly come a day when you will be reunited with that precious child and spend eternity together. Until then, please lift your head. Lift your heart. Let Me show you that life has a purpose, even on this side of such deep grief.

Unique Grieving

. . . .

May our Lord Jesus Christ himself and God
our Father, who loved us and by his grace
gave us eternal encouragement and good hope,
encourage your hearts and strengthen
you in every good deed and word.

2 THESSALONIANS 2:16–17 NIV

No one grieves the same. A husband will suffer through loss differently than his wife. A child will have her own way of coping, and her moments of grieving might catch you off guard. I see into the heart of every hurting person, and I know how to minister love and hope to each individual. So please don't fret if your loved ones don't weep as you weep. Don't be anxious if you don't have the same feelings of despair that they have. In other words, don't compare. This isn't the time for that. I created you to be you, and your emotions are just as I designed. And just as I have the ability to bring healing to your heart, I can heal those you love as well. My grace brings eternal encouragement. It offers hope where there has been no hope. It strengthens at the very moment when you feel your weakest. More than anything, I long to see all My children come through the recovery process whole and healed. Be patient and watch My miraculous hand at work.

LOSS OF NORMAL

Humble yourselves, therefore, under God's mighty hand, that he may lift you up in due time. Cast all your anxiety on him because he cares for you.

1 PETER 5:6–7 NIV

You never say it out loud. You don't have to. But I get it: You wish your life were normal. You wish the days of caring for one in constant need were behind you, or that the load were somehow lightened. You wish you could go and do, as your friends are going and doing. You dream of the days when you can say yes instead of no and when the weight of responsibility is eased. My children grieve so many different things. I see your desire for a "normal" house, one where you can serve as hostess. You want pretty rooms filled with inviting things. You want clean. You want organized. You want new, fresh, pretty. Instead, you feel stuck. And because you're stuck, you don't want to open your doors to those you love. I encourage you to start today. Make a plan. I'll help you. Together, we can put things in their proper order. Along the way I will settle your heart and whisper words of hope. Things will be good again, but they will never be the normal you once knew. They'll be far, far greater. Just trust Me and watch as that promise comes to pass.

CRASHING WAVES

· ·

For Christ also suffered once for sins,
the righteous for the unrighteous, that he might
bring us to God, being put to death in the
flesh but made alive in the spirit.

1 PETER 3:18 ESV

Grief has washed over you for a while now. You wonder if it will pull you under completely, like the surf dragging you beneath the rough, salty waves. You can barely keep your head above water these days. The risk of drowning feels imminent. You long for the days when your feet touched the ground, when you could gasp for breath and actually feel oxygen entering your lungs. I want to come to your rescue, My child. I want to lift you above the waves and help you catch your breath. I want to regain your trust and place your feet on solid ground, far from the rocky ups and downs. But you have to stop fighting Me. As hard as it might be, relax and let Me intervene. The battle is so much harder when you try to handle it on your own. You need My intervention today, and you'll need it again tomorrow. . .and that's okay. I love you, and I'll walk across the tumultuous waves to rescue you, even while the storm rages on every side. That's how much I care.

SUICIDE

. . . .

For no one is cast off by the Lord forever.
Though he brings grief, he will show compassion,
so great is his unfailing love. For he does not
willingly bring affliction or grief to anyone.

LAMENTATIONS 3:31–33 NIV

I have come that My children would have life, and yet your family is experiencing an unexpected and tragic death, one that makes no sense at all. Your loved one has taken her life. And with that, she's taken every ounce of strength from you and from all who loved her. You're left confused, broken, gut-sick, and questioning everything you said and did in those final days and weeks. You fight to come up with the proper words whenever a friend or loved one asks that awful question: How did she die? You don't want to tell them. . .and I don't blame you. Suicide was never part of My plan for mankind. I understand why you're feeling robbed, cheated, and confused. Today I'm here to remind you that your loved one's decision was not a result of anything you said or did. Brokenness and pain paved the way to this heartbreaking end, but you were not the one responsible. There is a very real enemy, and he works overtime to steal, kill, and destroy. You can't let him take what's left of your hope right now. Experience My compassion. Rest in My love. As horrible as this season is, I can—and *will*—bring peace.

UNWANTED

. . . .

*"I will not leave you as orphans;
I will come to you."*

JOHN 14:18 NIV

There is a grief so deep that it cannot be seen with the human eye or expressed with mere words. It's one that few of My children even fully understand. It's the grief of not being wanted by someone you love. I've watched you struggle—wishing, hoping, praying that person would eventually come around and love you as you have loved him. Surely one day he will respond as you hope. I sense your feelings of failure and hear you whispering that you will never measure up. Oh, how you try to please this person! How hard you work! How diligent you are! I want you to know—I need you to know—that *I* want you. I want you in a way that's deeper, stronger, more tender than any you'll experience from a human being (parent, spouse, or closest friend). I don't just want you; I love you and want to spend time with you. As any good father needs a relationship with his child, I need time with you. So shift your gaze. Instead of working, working, working to prove yourself worthy to an individual, turn to Me. Stop working. Rest in My presence and know that you are loved and wanted, just as you are. Oh, how I adore you!

VALLEY OF GRIEF

Even though I walk through the darkest
valley, I will fear no evil, for you are with me;
your rod and your staff, they comfort me.

PSALM 23:4 NIV

Oh, how I understand! You want to hold your loved one's hand again. You want to hear the sound of his laughter, to gaze into his eyes, to see the twinkle that once lit his face. You want to look with joy at that familiar smile as it spreads across his face, and you long to hear the jovial laughter in his voice as he shares a story or a joke. Instead, all you feel is pain, a pain that cuts so deep that you wonder if you'll ever recover. You've come to understand the phrase "valley of the shadow," though you wish you weren't familiar with it at all. Anything would be better than this dark place, filled with shadowy twists and turns. I beg you to shift your gaze, to look to Me. And even though it might not seem possible in the moment, please let Me convince you that you will find comfort and peace on the other side of this valley of grief. I promise, you will eventually be able to look up and see slivers of sunlight from above. I'll send hope, and it will not disappoint. Then, with our hands firmly clasped, I will lead you out of this valley and into the light.

STILLBIRTH

*" 'He will wipe every tear from their eyes.
There will be no more death' or mourning
or crying or pain, for the old order
of things has passed away."*

REVELATION 21:4 NIV

Horrific. That's the only word you can come up with. You've spent months with this infant in your womb. This baby has been all you've dreamed about, all you've hoped for. Tiny clothes are hanging in the closet, in perfect order. The room is decorated with all the things a baby would love. A name is chosen, one that has special significance to you. And now, for absolutely no reason that you can understand, your baby has been taken from you—ripped from your heart, from your arms. A life ended so abruptly that it feels like a terrible dream. I understand the pain of losing a child, dear one. Oh, how I understand. The shock is an awful thing to bear. But I will help you through even this, the hardest season of your life. There will come a day when that child will leap into your arms. When you reach heaven's shore, a reuniting will take place that will make your heart sing. Until then, I will hold you in My arms and speak words of comfort and peace. Don't give up. There will be joyous days ahead, even though it may seem impossible to believe now. Your darling child is safe in My care, arms outstretched, dancing in glorious praise.

Frozen

. . . .

" *'I will give you a new heart and put a new spirit in you; I will remove from you your heart of stone and give you a heart of flesh.' "*

EZEKIEL 36:26 NIV

My children are all so very different. Some express their grief, their emotions, openly. They weep; they share their feelings with friends and loved ones. Others hide it all away, their emotions locked up in a heart that feels completely frozen. I understand. To open yourself up to the pain—to acknowledge it, to ask the tough "Why, Lord?" questions—would be too hard. But I long for that frozen heart of yours to melt so that we can be real with each other. Won't you allow Me to begin the heart-thawing process? I want to replace that emptiness you feel with life—full, abundant life—but this requires a warming process. I can handle the hard questions, and I will respond out of My Word and through My Spirit. I won't leave you hanging, wondering if you're alone. But first you have to let Me soften your heart. Only when it reaches the melting point will I be able to do the necessary work to bring complete healing.

WEANING BABY

· ·

"Do what seems best to you," her husband Elkanah told her. "Stay here until you have weaned him; only may the LORD make good his word." So the woman stayed at home and nursed her son until she had weaned him.

1 SAMUEL 1:23 NIV

᚛᚛᚛᚛᚛

I designed you to love your baby with your whole heart and have equipped you with all the nutrition a newborn would need for the first few months of life. How you've loved nursing him. And how he has loved gazing up into his mama's eyes filled with love and tenderness. This precious season has bonded the two of you and set the stage for a relationship that will last the rest of your lives. But that little one is growing and changing. What was sufficient today will be insufficient tomorrow. You've sensed it for a while now but haven't wanted things to change. Still, the time has come to wean that little one. You're grieving that notion, but I celebrate it, because I see your child's growth and transition into the person I've created him to be. The seasons of your baby's life are beautifully laid out by Me, from conception forward, and this is just one of the turns in the road that you will face as he grows. There will be plenty of "weanings" ahead—as he lets go of your hand to ride a bike, as he climbs onto the school bus for the first time, as he leaves home for college, as he takes a bride. . . This is just the beginning, Mama. Let's make this first big transition together.

Out of Sync

> "*Your eye is the lamp of your body. When your eyes are healthy, your whole body also is full of light. But when they are unhealthy, your body also is full of darkness.*"
>
> LUKE 11:34 NIV

For a while now, you've been out of sync, haven't you? You're not taking care of yourself. You're skipping showers. Sitting in dark rooms. Hiding under the covers. Things feel pointless. Numbness has taken over. And how cruel the world around you seems! It's as if nature hasn't gotten the memo that you're in agony. The sun keeps on shining. People keep on enjoying their lives. Cars keep zipping along the roads. Life goes on. You sometimes wonder if you'll ever get back in sync again, if you'll join the land of the living. The proverbial cogs in the wheel of your life feel "off," out of place. I want to change your vision, child. When your eyes are in alignment with what I'm doing, your heart will follow. So look to Me. I'll give you the proper vision to escape this pit you're in. If you trust Me, if you put your hand in Mine, I will perform a mighty work in your life. Before long, the cogs will be perfectly aligned once more. Things will function more smoothly. Getting to that point will take work, but we'll do it together. I promise.

Mourning the Holidays

. . . .

Then all the people went away to eat and drink,
to send portions of food and to celebrate with
great joy, because they now understood the
words that had been made known to them.

NEHEMIAH 8:12 NIV

Those around you are celebrating. The holidays have everyone in a cheerful frame of mind. But your heart is breaking in two. Oh, you're doing your best to hide it. Why bring others down, especially during a joyous season like this? Still, I see past the strained smile you've plastered on your face. I know that you're trying to hide the pain. The searing ache of missing your loved one during what should be a joyous season is getting to you. You've forced your way through many hard days like this one—Christmas, Thanksgiving, Mother's Day, a birthday, even the anniversary of your loved one's death. Others don't see the pain you've buried so deep inside, but I do. I want to use these special days to bring sweet memories that will last a lifetime. I'm not trying to cause pain, but neither do I want you to forget your loved one. So remember the Christmas memories from days gone by. Celebrate the birthdays with a special cake or card. But don't let the pain of what you once had cloud the joy of what I'm bringing your way today. Your loved one wouldn't want that, and neither do I.

BROKEN FATHERS

*Fathers, do not exasperate your children;
instead, bring them up in the training
and instruction of the Lord.*

EPHESIANS 6:4 NIV

You have grieved deeply over father-daughter issues. I
see that. Your earthly father has let you down, time and
time again. He's overlooked you, hurt you, even wounded
you with words or deeds. Worst of all, he doesn't see the
problem. He doesn't acknowledge his actions, nor does
he seem to care. You've filed his indiscretions away in a
cabinet in your heart, one locked with a key so deeply
hidden that no one else—other than Me—can find it.
Every heartache is in there. Every betrayal. Every lost
hope, dream, vision. . . It's time to hand Me the key, sweet
child. What your earthly father could not accomplish I
will do through the Spirit. I'll be there at every event.
I'll speak words of encouragement and hope, even when
you make mistakes (as all children do). I'll make you feel
wanted and loved, never overlooked. I will never hurt you
or cause you pain. I will never cause you grief. In short,
I'll be the dad you never had. We'll grow our relationship
into a thing of beauty; and you will see, once and for all,
what a real Father-daughter bond looks like.

BOOTSTRAPS

. . . .

"Call to me and I will answer you,
and will tell you great and hidden things
that you have not known."

JEREMIAH 33:3 ESV

They keep telling you to be strong, to pull up your bootstraps and do what you have to do to keep moving forward. (As if things were really that easy!) They don't understand how hard this is for you, how complicated your emotional response to this loss has been. They don't see that you're not doing well, psychologically or physically. You feel guilty for not meeting the expectations of your friends and family, but how can you, with your heart broken in two? How can you possibly rejoin the land of the living when you're going through so much pain? You're weary with pretending. I see that. So the grief slips out—again and again. Those who love you don't seem to understand your method of grieving this loss, but I do. They want you to get over it quickly. Quietly. Me? I'm far more compassionate in approach. I long for you to rest in Me, to trust that I can take that raw grief and add My healing salve. Don't get hung up on what others are thinking or expecting. Just look to Me. Together, we can get through this. Together, we can move forward, no bootstraps involved.

LOSS OF PARENTS

. . . .

Precious in the sight of the LORD is the death of his faithful servants.

PSALM 116:15 NIV

Your parents taught you everything. . .except how to live without them. Now you're navigating that journey on your own, without their input. The family unit, as you once knew it, has been through a shift, a shaking. Family gatherings won't be the same without that special one there. You're the "elder" now, but that idea doesn't seem to fit the picture in your head. Nothing feels grounded. Nothing feels right. The loss of your parent dredges up a variety of emotions: love, remembrance, tenderness, despair, joy, and regret. Suffering has ceased for your parent, but you're in deep agony. Oh, how I long to bring comfort during this difficult season. I want to help you keep the memories alive, but I also want to see you healed from the pain. Why? In part, because you need to move forward for the sake of the whole family. Many are looking to you now. So put your hand in Mine. I'll guide you on this precarious journey as you move into the next season of life. And though things will never be the same, new memories will be made, new joys experienced.

STAGES OF A CHILD'S GROWTH

"All your children will be taught by the LORD, and great will be their peace."

ISAIAH 54:13 NIV

Life moves in stages, each one ordained by Me. There's a time to be born, a time to have your every need cared for by others, and a time to let go and spread your own wings. That baby you're holding in your arms? That sweet child will look a lot different a year from now, and she will continue to morph—internally and externally—as the years go by. Don't fret, Mama! "Different" isn't bad. Don't grieve the changes too much. In fact, I would encourage you to get used to them. There will be plenty more ahead. Before long, she'll be in school, then trying out for the Christmas pageant at church. She'll be primping for her first date, dressing for the senior prom, and taking her place with other new moms when her first child is born. It's impossible to imagine all those things right now, of course, but they will happen. And she'll need you—her mom—to guide her every step of the way. So don't spend too much time grieving the changes. You've got work to do, Mom.

BEHIND YOU. . .OR BEFORE YOU?

Brothers and sisters, I do not consider myself yet to have taken hold of it. But one thing I do: Forgetting what is behind and straining toward what is ahead, I press on toward the goal to win the prize for which God has called me heavenward in Christ Jesus.

PHILIPPIANS 3:13–14 NIV

I see what's happened. You've been blindsided by grief. It makes no sense. Time has passed. . .*a lot* of time. You thought the grieving was behind you. Others said it should be done, that it would tuck itself into a drawer, never to be dealt with again. And yet, here you are, wondering why it all feels so fresh, so painful. Something has triggered these feelings, and the emotions have caught you off guard. You've been pounced on unexpectedly. Don't be too hard on yourself. This happens to all My children from time to time. Memories have a way of rising to the surface when you least expect them. Don't let them overwhelm you. Take a deep breath. Let these unexpected moments bring comfort, not pain. Before long, that grief will slip away once more, hiding itself in the drawer. It won't stay put forever, of course; but when it rises to the surface next time, you'll be ready for it.

EMPTY NEST

"The LORD your God is with you, the Mighty Warrior who saves. He will take great delight in you; in his love he will no longer rebuke you, but will rejoice over you with singing."

ZEPHANIAH 3:17 NIV

Your little birdies have flown the nest, and your heart feels empty. Confused. The rooms of your home, once full, now echo—the emptiness causing physical pain as you draw in each breath. What a strange and unpredictable transition this is! Memories overtake you, and you wonder if you will adjust to this new normal. You knew it was coming, of course. You tried to prepare yourself. But this empty-nest thing is harder than you expected.

Oh, My child, you will adjust! I'm "delighting" over you during this season, singing a brand-new song over your life. Before long, you will no longer grieve the quiet. You will find new ways to spread your own wings. You'll fly as never before and experience new joys. You'll still love those kiddos as much as ever but will appreciate your freedom as you soar to new heights and try different things. Don't be surprised at the doors I plan to open for you. Just be ready to sail through them when the time comes. You can do this, mama bird!

Living a Lie

Deliver my soul, O LORD,
from lying lips, from a deceitful tongue.

PSALM 120:2 NASB

Someone you know and love has been living a lie. She's
not who she claimed to be. The truth has surfaced, and it's
like a kick in the gut. Everything you thought you knew
is false. You feel like a fool. You've been bamboozled.
You've been taken for a ride, one you never cared to go
on. And now the experience has knocked the breath out
of you. *Betrayal* doesn't seem a strong enough word for
what has been done to you. You're grieving on multiple
levels. Grieving a person who didn't really exist. Grieving
a situation you can't fix. Grieving a person who's so lost
she doesn't even care about the pain she's caused. Oh,
how My heart goes out to you. My arms are here to wrap
around you, to bring comfort. And even in the midst of
the confusion and pain I want you to know that I'm not
like that. I am who I say I am. I will be who My Word says
I will be—both now and forever. I am not like humans.
I can't lie. So lean on Me. . .no one else. I won't let you
down. That's a promise you can count on.

INSIDE OUT

Do not conform to the pattern of this world,
but be transformed by the renewing of your mind.
Then you will be able to test and approve what
God's will is—his good, pleasing and perfect will.

ROMANS 12:2 NIV

You feel like your heart is twisting inside out. It's a horrible feeling, the hardest thing you've ever been through, and something you wouldn't wish on your worst enemy. The pain feels relentless. You cry until you're cried out. And then, just when you think it's impossible to cry anymore, off you go again, violent sobs overtaking you. I want you to know that I'm a God of the inside out. I like to get into the deep, dark places where the pain lives. I want to offer My balm, My ointment, to those deep wounds. I'll speak My words over the situation and give you My thoughts, My heart, My plan. It might seem impossible in the moment, but trust Me. I'm asking you not to conform to the world's way of thinking, even in this, the hardest of situations. Don't let grief consume you. Let Me transform your heart, your mind. Let Me show you that My will for your life—even during this broken and hurting season—is pleasing and perfect. Will you trust Me, child?

LOSS OF YOUTH

. . . .

*"Even to your old age and gray hairs I am he,
I am he who will sustain you. I have made
you and I will carry you; I will sustain
you and I will rescue you."*

ISAIAH 46:4 NIV

Oh, to be young again! I hear those words rolling around in your heart and mind on a daily basis. You long for the days when things seemed easier. Your body was in tip-top shape—vibrant and healthy in every regard. Your future seemed as bright and shiny as a copper penny. Now you grieve that once-small waistline and those once-firm upper arms. You wish you could spin backward in time. Oh, how I long for you to know the joy that comes with aging. It's part of My plan. I'll carry you; I'll deliver you; I'll hold you up as you go through changes. Your body might be morphing, but I'm not. I'm the same, yesterday, today, and tomorrow. And My feelings for you will never change, even as you age. I still look at you as the same beautiful daughter I've always known and loved. So don't long for yesterday or envy those who are younger. This next season of your life might include a few gray hairs, but you'll learn to love the wisdom that comes with age as you trust in Me.

Retirement

*Being confident of this very thing, that He who
has begun a good work in you will complete
it until the day of Jesus Christ.*

PHILIPPIANS 1:6 NKJV

You've waited for it, prayed for it, and now it's here: retirement. All you've waited for has finally come to pass. Those quiet, peaceful years when you can do what you want, when you want, and with whomever you want. . . they're right in front of you now. Why, then, is your countenance sad? Perhaps you're missing the days when you rushed off to work, hung out with your coworkers, went to lunch together, talked about world events with one another, debated politics. You miss the family environment of your workplace. I understand this, of course. I created you with a heart for relationships, but don't grieve, My child! I have plenty more planned for your future. And that's what you have ahead of you, you know. . .a bright and promising future. Your days of productivity aren't behind you. The setting of your story might be changing, but your effectiveness, your ability to help others? . . . Those things are as strong as ever. So settle in! Enjoy your retirement. And while you're at it, kick up those feet and rest a bit. You've certainly earned it!

How Long, O Lord?

. . . .

Then Joseph had a dream, and when he told it to his brothers, they hated him even more. He said to them, ". . .Behold, we were binding sheaves in the field, and lo, my sheaf rose up and also stood erect; and behold, your sheaves gathered around and bowed down to my sheaf." Then his brothers said to him, "Are you actually going to reign over us? Or are you really going to rule over us?" So they hated him.

GENESIS 37:5–8 NASB

You're filled with dreams. Longings. Wishes. Hopes. And you've been waiting a very long time for the fulfillment of those things, longer than most. You've watched as your friends and family members have met their goals. . .seen their wishes come true. Now you're reaching the giving-up point. Your heart is heavy every time you remember those once-fresh dreams. It's easier to close the door on the dream than to face the disappointment of not seeing it come to pass. And your friends and family aren't helping either. They don't understand. They aren't offering support. Don't give up hope! I bring all things to pass according to My perfect timing. Your day hasn't come yet, but that doesn't mean it won't. Keep dreaming. Keep speaking words of faith. And when you begin to see those dreams come true, you'll be so happy that you did not allow grief to consume you along the way. Big things are ahead, dear one!

CLEANSING STREAM

. . . .

Purge me with hyssop, and I shall be clean:
wash me, and I shall be whiter than snow.

PSALM 51:7 KJV

You're finding it difficult to put into words what you're feeling. I can see that. Grief has caked you, like murky mud. Stiff. Confining. It's squeezing the breath out of your once-healthy lungs and causing you to gasp for air. At times you feel you can't see, and you wonder if you will ever be able to dig your way out of this pit. You're longing for the day when your heart beats normally again and your lungs can grab adequate air to sustain your life. Oh, My child, let Me wash off that caked-on mud, once and for all. It has held you suspended long enough. Let Me free you up from the inside out. This is no way to live, bound up and constricted. I want you to breathe freely, to see past where you are now to where you will be. You are headed to a healthier place. I promise. You will get there. But you can't if you're locked in place. So step into My presence. You're about to experience a cleansing stream of mercy, grace, and love like you've never known.

HEALING FROM GRIEF

. . . .

> " 'Nevertheless, I will bring health and healing
> to it; I will heal my people and will let them
> enjoy abundant peace and security.' "

JEREMIAH 33:6 NIV

I hear the questions that go through your mind day after day: *Will I ever heal from this grief? Will the pain always cut this deep?* You're so tired of feeling sick inside. It feels like an endless cycle, circles and circles of pain. Grief runs in seasons, and there's no way for you to guess how long those seasons will last. But remember, My child, I created the seasons—even the cold, hard ones. I know, down to the millisecond, how long each one will last. None of them go on forever. (Isn't that a comforting thought?) Think about that for a moment. I know and I care. And because I care, I can promise you this: The pain you're feeling right now—that crippling, agonizing sensation that grips you when you least expect it—will go away in time. Your broken heart will, with My help, begin to piece itself back together. The scars that form will provide a barrier that will help you heal. And though it seems impossible at this moment, you will once again see the future as a bright and hopeful thing.

SEEK HELP

*"Ask, and it will be given to you; seek,
and you will find; knock, and it will
be opened to you."*

MATTHEW 7:7 NKJV

I see inside your heart, My child, and I know the troubling thoughts that go through your mind as well. You're struggling. This grief season has been hard on you. You're wondering where to turn for help or if you might be capable of receiving the kind of assistance you need. Who will understand? Who will have the right advice, the best plan to help you transition out of the pain? I have equipped many of My people for situations such as this. They have been trained and are standing by, ready to help. These godly people have the right words to share, the most beneficial ideas to help you move forward. They will guide you, pray for you, put their arms around you and offer encouragement. In short, they will help you heal and move beyond this painful season. So don't be afraid to ask for help. There will come a day when you will look back on this season and be so glad you did. And remember this: you will be able to offer the help you receive today to others tomorrow. Before long, people will be leaning on you, and you'll have gracious words of advice.

An Unwanted Package

. . . .

Why, my soul, are you downcast?
Why so disturbed within me? Put your hope
in God, for I will yet praise him,
my Savior and my God.

PSALM 42:11 NIV

❧

You've been handed a package you didn't order, one you didn't pay for or ever hope to possess. You've been handed grief, and it's an unwelcome gift, dumped into your arms, heavy and uncomfortable. And though you've attempted to unwrap it, to peer inside, it's just too painful. So you've carried it until your back aches and your shoulders slump forward in defeat. You would love to toss it aside but can't figure out how to do that. Is there a RETURN TO SENDER tag you can use, perhaps? You forge ahead, bent over, strained. This feels like a forever situation. I see how the weight is dragging you down. Today, I ask you to pass the weight you've been carrying into My capable hands. It will not be too much for Me to bear, I promise. Give it to Me. Release it. Free yourself to stand straight again, to look forward, not down. I'll blow away the ashes of despair if you will hand Me that package, child. Please don't wait a minute longer. I'm here. Waiting. See these hands? They're ready to carry that load.

Divorce

*He heals the brokenhearted
and binds up their wounds.*

PSALM 147:3 NIV

Dear one, I see your broken heart. It's been crushed. Bloodied. Abused. You gave your heart to another—one who pledged to love you *till death do us part*—and it did not end as you had hoped or prayed. Either he didn't really mean it or he changed his mind somewhere along the way. One flesh has been ripped in two, and now you wonder if you can ever trust anyone again. You also wonder if the grieving will ever end, if life will ever get back to normal. Are you half a person now? Will you ever be whole again? I want you to know that My heart is still forever linked to yours. I really will stick with you *till death do us part. . .* only death won't part us. It will bind us forever. You will spend eternity with Me, our love story outlasting the ages. So hang in there, girl of My heart. You will be whole once again, with My help. On that day the grieving will end. You will smile again. You'll be hopeful again. And our happily-ever-after will mean more to you than ever before. Trust Me. I promise I won't let you down.

LOSS OF CHOICE

"But if serving the LORD seems undesirable to you, then choose for yourselves this day whom you will serve, whether the gods your ancestors served beyond the Euphrates, or the gods of the Amorites, in whose land you are living. But as for me and my household, we will serve the LORD."

JOSHUA 24:15 NIV

Choice. It's a gift, isn't it? I love it when My kids make good choices. . .and you've made so many over the years. The best possible choice is the one to follow Me all the days of your life. It brings such joy to My heart when I see you make the choice to spend eternity with Me. But there are other choices to be made as well—daily, weekly, monthly, yearly. Tough choices. You've done a fine job with most of them, but I see where you're struggling with others. I also see that you sometimes feel as though you're out of choices. You feel like your hands are tied. You grieve the loss of freedom you once knew. When you face these seasons, please know that My ultimate joy is to see you walking in complete peace and freedom in Me. Do you trust Me? Then let Me help you make the best possible choices for your life.

LOST HOPE

. . . .

A happy heart makes the face cheerful,
but heartache crushes the spirit.

PROVERBS 15:13 NIV

The enemy of your soul has come to steal, to kill, and to destroy. There's a reason he's called a thief. He'll take anything and everything. The one thing he's most interested in stealing is your hope. You've got to be on guard, especially during the grieving seasons. Don't let him have your hope, dear one. Oh, he'll try to wrestle it out of your hands, but hold on tight. Hope is a lifeline that links you to Me. It keeps your eyes focused upward when troubles are tugging at you, threatening to pull you away. If you can hold on to hope, you can see tomorrow as doable. What is hope, you ask? It's the holy sense that anything could happen, despite the circumstances. Healing can come. Broken marriages can be healed. Wayward children can turn their hearts toward home. Hope is one of the most valuable treasures in your treasure chest, so guard it under lock and key. Don't let the naysayers rob you of it. Don't let negative circumstances tempt you to let go of it. Keep that spark of hope alive, no matter what.

UNEXPECTED

Precious in the sight of the LORD is the death of his faithful servants.

PSALM 116:15 NIV

Unexpected. That's the only word that comes to mind, isn't it? What has happened feels so unexpected, so out of the blue, so wholly and completely unfair. And now the grief has wrapped itself around you like a fog. It has cut you off from the outside world. You're unable to take care of yourself, to eat properly, to do normal, everyday things. That's what happens when the unexpected occurs. It makes everything seem completely out of place. But I am right here with you, My child. I promise. This situation didn't take Me by surprise. Neither has it shaken Me from My throne. I'm solid as a rock. And though you're feeling hollow and scared right now, I make a commitment to you that I won't leave you, even in the darkest hour. I'll send others to comfort you. They'll wrap their arms of love around you. Look for unexpected blessings from Me as you walk through this next season. There will be unexpected passages from My Word that jump out at you, too. In other words, I'll use the unexpected to turn this situation for the good.

OH, THOSE CHANGES

For You formed my inward parts; You wove me in my mother's womb. I will give thanks to You, for I am fearfully and wonderfully made; wonderful are Your works, and my soul knows it very well.

PSALM 139:13–14 NASB

I gave you emotions. Let Me repeat that: I gave you emotions. The ups, the downs, the all-arounds. . .they're all a gift from Me. I created you to laugh, to cry, to feel joy, to wonder, to stand in awe. I blessed you with the ability to release tears, to shout for joy, and to sigh with relief. These emotions are meant to be a blessing; and yet, I see when you're struggling with them. They go up; they plummet to the ground. They go up again, and so forth. This is particularly difficult when you're going through physical changes brought on by hormones (things like pregnancy, menopause, and so on). Do I want you to maintain some level of control? Of course. Do I understand the ups and downs? Certainly. I'll help you level out through this volatile season. You won't be left floundering. But you've got to keep your eyes on Me. Don't depend on how you feel. (Feelings will betray you.) Don't grieve the loss of the ups when you're down. And don't worry that the downs will last forever. They won't. Just trust that we'll get to the "ups" again. . .hand in hand.

LOSS OF A MENTOR

*The Israelites grieved for Moses in the plains
of Moab thirty days, until the time of
weeping and mourning was over.*

DEUTERONOMY 34:8 NIV

Oh, how I love placing mentors in your life. I know just
whom to pick because I know you so well. So I've chosen
the very ones to best pour into your life, your ministry,
and your heart. (Haven't they done a fine job?) I also love
using you as a mentor to others. These precious people
depend on you to learn and to grow, and you depend
on the relationships to bring fulfillment and joy. These
seasons don't last forever, of course. I see how much you
grieve when the various mentoring seasons come to an
end. People move away, life marches on, and you feel as
though those who have poured into you are far, far away.
Don't fear! Don't grieve! I've got other blessings ahead for
you, other friends who will speak into your life and bring
words of wisdom. And remember, I still plan to use you to
speak into the lives of others as well—perhaps even a few
people you haven't even met yet. Just trust Me. Mentoring
is My idea, after all. It will always play its role in your life.

DREAMS

. . . .

Every good and perfect gift is from above,
coming down from the Father of the heavenly
lights, who does not change like shifting shadows.

JAMES 1:17 NIV

I'm the dream planter. You're the dreamer (and a fine one, at that). We make a good team, you and I. Together, we've come up with some fabulous ideas, some real whoppers. (You're thinking about some of them right now, aren't you?) We've watched many come to fruition and a few peter out. And on the days like today when you begin to doubt that little seed of a dream in your heart, I'm here to water it and to bring it to fulfillment. You're not so sure it still works like that, though. You're discouraged, wondering why I don't get My act together and move on your behalf. It's really My timing you're doubting, isn't it? You would've had this thing wrapped up a long time ago. That's what a go-getter you are! You're beginning to lose heart because it's taking too long. You're disappointed in the plan and in Me. But I know the perfect time to make your dream a reality, and I'm waiting so that you can have the best possible outcome. So trust Me in the interim, okay? Keep that seed of hope alive. Keep on dreaming. Keep on believing. And don't grieve what hasn't really been lost.

Change of Address

. . . .

I will instruct you and teach you in the way
you should go; I will counsel you
with my loving eye on you.

Psalm 32:8 niv

Moving. . . I know it sounds frightening. Change isn't
easy. You've worked so hard to make everything perfect
in your current home, the place you love. The color
scheme. The yard. The new roof. The updated kitchen.
The new fireplace mantel. Oh, how you enjoyed every
task. You've made the place a thing of beauty. And now
you have to hand the keys to someone else who probably
won't even appreciate all the work you've put in. Hardly
seems fair. Trust Me when I say that this move will turn
out to be a blessing in the end. I'll be right there, every
step of the way. Yes, you're leaving a place that has felt
secure. Homey. And yes, heading into the unknown calls
for an adventurous spirit. But I thrive on adventure. So
don't mourn the loss of the old as you step into the new.
There will be plenty of walls to paint there, too. Plenty
of drapes to hang. Plenty of cabinets to replace. Just
enjoy the process, and trust that I have lovely things in
store for you.

GOOD FROM BAD

And we know that in all things God works for the good of those who love him, who have been called according to his purpose.

ROMANS 8:28 NIV

Your teenager has broken your heart. She's done something unimaginable, and the whole family is reeling. The disappointment is severe. You never expected this. Right now you're in cleanup mode. You want to extend grace but wonder if tough love would be the better approach. You're asking Me (several times a day) if anything good will come of this season. You're quoting My Word, especially that scripture from Romans 8 that you love so much. Oh, sweet daughter, trust Me. . .I know what it's like to be disappointed and grieved by a child's actions. You might recall a time or two when you wandered from Me as well. Didn't I turn things around? Haven't I always brought good from bad? That's what will happen this time, too. No matter how disappointed you are right now, no matter how bleak things look, I have a plan for your child's life, and I'm just on the cusp of revealing it. So don't give up. Wade your way through the heartache. And remember, I have big things ahead. Don't get bogged down in yesterday and lose sight of tomorrow.

GRIEVING CHILDREN

. . . .

*I remain confident of this: I will see the
goodness of the LORD in the land of the
living. Wait for the LORD; be strong
and take heart and wait on the LORD.*

PSALM 27:13–14 NIV

It's killing you. You're so tired of watching your child grieve.
He's been emotionally wounded, hurt by one he trusted.
Why did this have to happen now, at such a critical time
in his life? You're upset at the one who hurt him, but I can
see that you're angry at Me, too. I could have stopped this.
But I didn't. And now your child is disgusted with everyone and ready to give up. He's hiding behind a slammed
door, unable to function at the same level. You feel like
doing the same yourself. How you wish you could fix this
for him, make everything better. If only you had a giant
eraser. You'd wipe away the betrayal and the pain. Instead,
you try to give him new coping skills. You offer insight
and understanding. What a good parent you are! You're
bringing solace. Comfort. If you lean on Me, I can show
you how to speak words of life over your child so that he
will grow up healthy and strong. And this pain he's going
through? It's not permanent. There might be a few scars,
but he will recover, and so will you. I promise.

LOSS OF A CHURCH

I appeal to you, brothers and sisters, in the name of our Lord Jesus Christ, that all of you agree with one another in what you say and that there be no divisions among you, but that you be perfectly united in mind and thought.

1 CORINTHIANS 1:10 NIV

My idea of the perfect church? The one that comes together to worship Me, side by side, hand in hand, heart to heart. Oh, how I love to see My children dwell together in unity. Only, something has happened. There's been a rift that has split your church body down the middle. You're at a crossroads. You don't know if you should stay or go. The decision is finally made to move on to a new church home. You're transitioning from a place where you felt a sense of togetherness for so long. Will you ever feel that again? Don't grieve, My child. I have the perfect home for you. You will find it and eventually settle in. I might need to do a little work in your heart first, though, so that you can forgive those from your former church home who've wounded you or made mistakes in judgment. I'm still a God of restoration, and that means I long for hearts to be mended and love to flow, even during difficult seasons. Only then will you find complete peace in your new church home. Trust Me? Good. We've got some work to do.

Aging Body

And even when I am old and gray, O God,
do not forsake me, until I declare Your
strength to this generation, Your power
to all who are to come.

PSALM 71:18 NASB

You're feeling your age, aren't you? The aching joints. The stiff back. The gray hairs. I see you thumbing through those photos from years gone by. There's a part of you, in your deepest heart of hearts, that wishes you still had that younger body. That shiny long hair. That boisterous energy. Those cellulite-free thighs. You'd take them back in an instant, if offered. Oh, but you are exactly where I've created you to be at this age and stage. I haven't abandoned you or left you to wither away. I still have so many amazing things for you to accomplish. Don't let the aging body stop you. Look around you. See those people your age and older? Many are up and at 'em, accomplishing great things. They're impacting lives. You can do the same. Sure, your body is different from what it once was, but never underestimate your ability or your effectiveness. I've created you in My image, after all. Now, shake off those doldrums and get to work!

MINISTRY OPPORTUNITY LOSSES

*Brothers and sisters, I do not consider myself
yet to have taken hold of it. But one thing I do:
Forgetting what is behind and straining toward
what is ahead, I press on toward the goal
to win the prize for which God has
called me heavenward in Christ Jesus.*

PHILIPPIANS 3:13–14 NIV

I see that heart of yours. You want to minister to others
with the gifts I've planted inside of you. You want to be
used to affect others for My kingdom, and that's a good
thing. Only now you feel like your opportunity has passed.
You wonder if that door will ever open again. Are your
ministry days behind you, or is this just an off-season?
I want you to know that you're not just usable—you're
strategically gifted to minister. I gave you those gifts. That
desire to help others? I put it there. That prompting to
do more for the kingdom? That's My prompting. And it
will come to pass in My timing. I promise. So don't worry
about this next phase. I'll get you to where you need to
go. And when you get there, you'll be amazed at all the
opportunities to spread your wings and fly. For now, pray.
Accept My peace. And prepare yourself for something
bigger than even you could have dreamed.

GRIEF OVER REBELLION

. . . .

*As has just been said: "Today, if you hear
his voice, do not harden your hearts
as you did in the rebellion."*

HEBREWS 3:15 NIV

Oh, how rebellion hurts My heart. I can see that it hurts
yours, too. You've grieved for hours over the rebellious
nature of someone you care about, someone who should
know better. You don't know what to do for him. You've
already tried so many things, but they all failed. Should
you extend grace or toughen your stance? Should you
chase him down, insist he obey? Should you step back
and trust that he will come around in time? Your thoughts
shift from moment to moment as your emotions get
involved. Pause for a moment and listen to My thoughts
about this special person, the one you love so much. I'll
show you what to do. Don't be impulsive. Don't be angry.
Trust that I will show you the way. And while you can't
control someone else's actions, you will learn how to pray
and how to respond so that the situation becomes less
volatile. How do I know? Because I've been down this
road with a few stubborn people Myself! I'm a big God. I
can—and will—speak to his heart. If his ears are full of
words from you, he'll have a harder time hearing. Trust
Me? Great. I'll take it from here.

A Friend in Need

A friend loves at all times,
and a brother is born for a time of adversity.

PROVERBS 17:17 NIV

Your friend is grieving. She's suffered a terrible loss, one that has ripped her heart in two. You wish you could help. You're praying for her—and that's a great start, but you want to do more. If only you could think of something that would make a difference. Start by wrapping your arms around her and letting her tears fall on your shoulder. Then tell her that you care deeply about what she's going through. Cry with her, if you feel so inclined. Let her share stories about her loss. Then take her by the hand and walk with her through this next season. She will likely vacillate from anger to tears to depression, but you can—with My help—be Me with skin on. That's what she needs more than anything right now, a reminder that I'm still here, I still care. And I do. Very much. That's why I've put you in exactly the place you're in. You are a friend who loves at all times, in good seasons and bad. It's time to make yourself available as never before.

Outside the Natural Order

*But everything should be done
in a fitting and orderly way.*

1 Corinthians 14:40 niv

There's a natural order to things. I created the universe to operate in a rhythmic and orderly fashion. . .everything flowing in perfect timing and harmony. When tragic losses occur, they feel "outside" the natural order. This is especially true when you face a devastating shock, like the death of a child or loved one. The young ones aren't supposed to go first. The sorrow that occurs during these unnatural losses is real and intense. You cry out, "His life had barely begun!" or "She was such a good person." These are legitimate and real observations. I want you to know that I care deeply about the pain you're going through as you witness these "out-of-order" losses. I understand the anger. I know you feel as though you've been robbed. It breaks My heart, too. I wish that sin and death had never entered the picture. I, too, long for the day when there will be no more death or suffering. A day is coming when we'll spend eternity together in a place that functions perfectly. . .all things in perfect order. Won't that be a wonderful day?

GRIEVING WHAT FEELS INEVITABLE

· ·

The LORD is my rock, my fortress and my deliverer; my God is my rock, in whom I take refuge, my shield and the horn of my salvation, my stronghold.

PSALM 18:2 NIV

It feels inevitable. Change is coming, and you're already grieving though it hasn't even arrived yet. You can sense it, though, and you've already got a knot in your stomach as you anticipate what's around the bend. What will the changes look like? How will they feel? Will this crippling sensation of being stuck between two places you don't belong ever end? Do you want it to end? Wouldn't it be easier to stay put than to plow forward into the unknown? Though transitions are hard, though grieving will take place, I will walk with you from one life experience to another. Don't equate the word *inevitable* with "terrible." It doesn't have to be, especially if I'm the One leading the way. Have I ever let you down? Trust Me. Even when you don't know what's coming. *Especially* when you don't know what's coming. I can see around that next bend even when you can't, and I've got good news for you: you're not only going to survive; you're going to thrive!

Fallen Ministers

. . . .

*No, I strike a blow to my body and make it
my slave so that after I have preached to others,
I myself will not be disqualified for the prize.*

1 Corinthians 9:27 niv

You've placed your trust in someone—a minister of the
Gospel, no less—and he has let you down. You're sick over
it. In fact, you didn't want to believe it at first. But it's true.
He has fallen from grace and you're left wondering how this
godly man—one you trusted as a spiritual leader—could
possibly have tumbled so low. The grief over his actions has
sent you (and hundreds of others) reeling. How will you
recover, as an individual or as a church body? Oh, there is
hope! Let Me remind you that I am a God of restoration.
I long to bring all My children to repentance and to see
My Church healthy and whole. Even now I'm working in
the life and heart of that fallen leader. With My help, he
can be restored. Sure, his situation might never look the
same, but I can bring good out of bad. So pray for him.
Pray that he lays down the facade and gets real with Me.
And while you're at it, pray for your church body as well.
Instead of wasting time talking about the one who's hurt
you, speak words of faith over the situation and watch
things improve.

LOSS OF A PARENT

. . . .

To every thing there is a season, and a time to every purpose under the heaven: a time to be born, and a time to die; a time to plant, and a time to pluck up that which is planted; a time to kill, and a time to heal; a time to break down, and a time to build up; a time to weep, and a time to laugh; a time to mourn, and a time to dance.

ECCLESIASTES 3:1–4 KJV

Oh, that heart! I see it breaking, and I understand. You've watched someone you love—someone who cared for you, nurtured you, met your needs—step from this life into another. You've got questions. *Why did it have to happen so soon? Why did he struggle so much? Didn't he deserve a better ending? What could I have done differently? Why do my friends still have their parents and mine were taken from me?* You're not sure what to think or feel during this difficult season. Just know that I'm here. I was holding you as you released the hand of your loved one into Mine, and I will go on holding you as you navigate these next few weeks and months without him. Don't ever forget how much I love the one you've lost. I have all of eternity to prove it. One day you'll see for yourself. . .but for now, just trust Me.

LOSS OF A PET

. . . .

The righteous care for the needs of their animals,
but the kindest acts of the wicked are cruel.

PROVERBS 12:10 NIV

Not everyone understands the love you had for your pet, but I do. All of creation was My idea, after all. I adore all creatures great and small—from domesticated animals to those roaming the wild. That sweet pet you've loved for so long was My special gift, just for you. I knew you would be friends, and I planned this special relationship to bring you great joy. And now your joy has turned to pain as you've had to say good-bye. My heart hurts for you because I see how great this loss truly is. During this season I encourage you to look around at all of nature, here for your enjoyment and pleasure. Don't grieve for too long. Peek at the kittens through the window at the pet store. Wave to your neighbor's poodle staring at you from the front window of the house. And open your heart to what's coming next. I will prepare you for just the right time, just the right darling pet to enter your home for the next season of life. Until then, just know how much I care.

Fractured Relationships

*Make every effort to keep the unity
of the Spirit through the bond of peace.*

She won't speak to you. You don't know why. What started as something small and trivial has morphed into a misunderstanding of epic proportions. You've tried everything to mend the relationship, but stubbornness on the other end prevails. Your e-mails go unanswered, the text messages ignored. Your heart is broken, but she doesn't seem to care. Not that you can tell how she's feeling. The only emotion you're sensing is anger. How can you fix this? What can be done to take things back to how they once were? The walls are too high to climb. The words too terse to be spoken. Her heart is too hard to soften. Will you live the rest of your life without this precious person acknowledging you, spending time with you, or enjoying life together as in years past? My heart breaks alongside yours. I cannot abide alienation. Walls between loved ones are not My idea, nor can I put My stamp of approval on them. I'm working extra hard to soften her heart, to tear down those walls, and I hope you'll keep praying to that end. Pray for restoration. Above all, trust that I haven't given up on this relationship. . .and never will.

THE THINGS THEY LOVED

*For no one is cast off by the Lord forever.
Though he brings grief, he will show compassion,
so great is his unfailing love. For he does not
willingly bring affliction or grief to anyone.*

LAMENTATIONS 3:31–33 NIV

You've lost a loved one, and now you're saddened every time you see, taste, or smell something that she once loved. Mint chocolate chip ice cream. Saltwater taffy. A particular brand of perfume. Sparkling Christmas lights. These are the things that remind you of your loss, and you can't control when or how they will surface. Neither can you seem to control the tears that come with each fresh trigger. Want to know a little secret? I don't want you to forget. I want you to remember the things your loved one loved, to be transported back in time, to celebrate the life of the one who's now gone. And I want your children, grandchildren, loved ones, and friends to one day remember all the things you love, too. This is one very special way to keep the legacy going. So don't be too sad the next time you see those candies your loved one couldn't live without. Don't be caught off guard. Instead, buy a bag for yourself and take a little nibble to keep the memory alive.

HEAVEN IS FOR REAL

"My Father's house has many rooms; if that were not so, would I have told you that I am going there to prepare a place for you?"

JOHN 14:2 NIV

Your loved one has transitioned from this life to heaven, and you feel completely lost. I see you, reaching for your phone, wishing you could call him for a quiet conversation. It's instinctive. He was always your first call, after all. Oh, the hours you spent, laughing and talking through life's problems. But there's no cheerful voice on the other end of the line. You listen to his voicemail again and again, just to hear his voice. I see you wandering the hallways of your house, wondering if you'll ever see him again. I want to remind you—though I'm sure you already know—that heaven is for real. A day is coming when a holy reuniting will take place. You will not just see those loved ones again; you'll spend eternity with them. When you reach that point, this season you're currently walking through will feel like a blink of an eye—just a tiny blip of time. So keep your eyes focused on heaven. We will be one big happy family, filled with love, laughter, and the ultimate in happily-ever-afters.

INABILITY TO WORK

May the favor of the Lord our God rest on us; establish the work of our hands for us— yes, establish the work of our hands.

PSALM 90:17 NIV

I know what a go-getter you are. You love to stay busy. Your calendar is full, your to-do list never ending. This is how I've wired you, to get things done. You're in your element when your plate is full. Only the plate is empty now. Your health issues have forced you into a position where you don't have the stamina, the energy, or the time to give to those projects you used to love. I see the struggle inside of your heart during this rough season. You're questioning yourself and those around you, wondering if you still have worth. Wondering if people will forget all the things you once accomplished. Will people find value in you anymore, now that you're unable to work like before? Troubling thoughts overtake you. You grieve the quiet, seemingly empty spaces. There are seasons for everything, as you've already learned. I'll give you a different kind of work to do that brings a sense of fulfillment. When the time is right, of course. Right now I'm focused on getting you well. In the meantime, hang out with Me. Rest. Listen to My heartbeat. Stay close. Pretty soon you'll be busy again, and I'll miss you as you race here, there, and everywhere.

Natural Disasters

. . . .

Brothers and sisters, we do not want you to be uninformed about those who sleep in death, so that you do not grieve like the rest of mankind, who have no hope.

1 Thessalonians 4:13 niv

The word *disaster* is a hard one to hear and an even harder one to bear. When you go through disasters—natural or otherwise—your body goes into shock. In its own way, shock is the body's way of protecting you. Even after the dust settles, it's often hard to fathom what just happened, because disasters most often strike out of the blue. The losses can be devastating. The mess. . .unthinkable. I see you glancing to the heavens, as if to ask, *Where were You, God? Why didn't You stop this?* You might not believe Me, but I was there in the very middle of the storm. I'm always there. And when great loss occurs as a result of the disaster, I can fill those empty spaces and make them whole again. I am a God of restoration. I make all things new again. This is My commitment to you. New life is coming. New days are coming. Fresh provision is coming. Trust Me. . . and wait on My Word to come true.

KIDS IN COLLEGE

. . . .

But thanks be to God! He gives us the victory through our Lord Jesus Christ. Therefore, my dear brothers and sisters, stand firm. Let nothing move you. Always give yourselves fully to the work of the Lord, because you know that your labor in the Lord is not in vain.

1 CORINTHIANS 15:57–58 NIV

You've helped him pack his bags. You've put your stamp of approval on his new dorm room, even helped purchase the necessary items like bedding, decor, and so forth. You've paid his tuition, purchased high-priced textbooks, filled the car tank with gas, and asked your prayer partners to join you in praying for your kiddo's safety. But leaving him at college? I saw how you grieved that. You wondered if life would ever go back to normal, if you would ever get over not hearing his voice as he hollered down the front hallway or smelling his sneakers when he left them in the laundry room. Remember, this is just a season. And it's a season that I can use greatly. You've done a fantastic job of raising your child and sending him out into the world. Now it's time to trust that I'll take it for the next little while. Is your work done? Absolutely not! Can you let go of the reins a little and trust Me? If so, you'll find that the next few years might just be the best few years for you as well.

LOSS OF SELF

. . . .

The heart of the wise is in the house of mourning,
but the heart of fools is in the house of pleasure.

ECCLESIASTES 7:4 NIV

Sometimes it feels like you're losing sight of yourself, doesn't it? You get so caught up in doing what others want (or need) that you feel a little lost. Your days don't even feel like they belong to you at all. So many hours are spent driving here and there, taking care of the needs and wants of those under your care. Occasionally, in the quiet of the night, you're reminded of the things you had hoped and planned to do with your life. You wonder if those things will ever come to pass. Then you wake up the next morning and dive back into your routine, caring for others, making sure their needs are met. You have to keep going for the sake of all who count on you. Remember, I created you to be compassionate and caring, but your day is coming, too. Instead of grieving the loss of who you might have been (and what you might have accomplished), spend time with Me for revelation. There's still plenty of time for you. You have not been overlooked. I have great plans for the days and years ahead.

Incarceration

. . . .

Blessed is the man who remains steadfast under
trial, for when he has stood the test he will
receive the crown of life, which God
has promised to those who love him.

JAMES 1:12 ESV

It doesn't seem real. Someone you love, someone you've cared for, has been incarcerated. His actions have led to a separation that breaks your heart. How can you stand being apart for so long? The idea of not being able to communicate is killing you. Will your loved one learn the necessary lessons? How can you best offer support and encouragement? I understand what it's like for those I love to be imprisoned. Many of My children choose to live their lives in bondage, addicted to drugs, alcohol, pornography, and a host of other things. It's heartbreaking to watch someone you adore bend to the will of others and relinquish who they really are, who they were created to be. The very best thing you can do right now is to pray. Pray for blind eyes to be opened. Pray for the bondage to be broken. And pray for your loved one's heart to be softened toward Me so that I can do the work that will forever change his circumstances, once and for all. This season of separation could just turn out to be the very best, because I'll finally have a chance to speak to your loved one's heart without the voices of his cohorts drowning out My voice. I'm on the move. Just wait and see.

Unexpected Pregnancy

. . . .

*"A woman giving birth to a child has pain because
her time has come; but when her baby is born
she forgets the anguish because of her joy
that a child is born into the world."*

JOHN 16:21 NIV

Babies are a wonderful gift from Me. Each one has a special
purpose and plan, but not every child is conceived under
the best of circumstances. Right now you're grieving
because someone you love—a teenage daughter, a single
friend—has just told you that she's expecting. You're
shocked. You're trying to figure out how she will manage.
She was in no way prepared for this. You wonder if she
will be able to adapt to do all that will be required. Will
you play a role? Will you help with the baby? If so, what
will that look like? How can you manage your already
full schedule and help with an infant? It's a lot to take in.
Sweet daughter, I'm here to remind you that every baby
is a blessing. Yes, you're in shock. Yes, there are decisions
to be made. But please remember that this little life did
not take Me by surprise. Sure, it came as a shock to you,
but not to Me. I will be here, every step of the way. I'm a
good Daddy who will love that little one, just as I love all
My kids. So brace yourself. We'll work together as a team
to give this child the very best life possible.

DOES TIME HEAL?

*"Then shall your light break forth like the
dawn, and your healing shall spring up speedily;
your righteousness shall go before you;
the glory of the LORD shall
be your rear guard."*

ISAIAH 58:8 ESV

"Time will heal your wounds," they tell you. "Just wait it
out." And so you wait. And wait. And wait some more.
Only, you're still not over it. You can't seem to stop hurting
whenever you think of all you've lost. The grief is as fresh
as if it just happened. I have an eternal truth for you, My
child: Time does not heal all wounds. *I* do. I'm the Great
Physician. I'm the One who will calm a broken heart and
bind up the broken places. I will perform heart surgery
when you feel mortally wounded. I will bring comfort
during those middle-of-the-night hours when you feel like
you're all alone. So don't worry about how long healing
takes. When you get to heaven, there will be no clocks.
No pressure to hurry up and get over anything. Time will
be meaningless in light of eternity. It's time to go ahead
and consider your current situation in that same light,
daughter. Today's struggles will feel like a tiny blink—just
a wink in time—when you see them from heaven's side.

BIRTHDAY CANDLES

. . . .

"But now he is dead. Why should I fast? Can I bring him back again? I shall go to him, but he will not return to me."

2 SAMUEL 12:23 ESV

Today's the day. Your little one—the baby who didn't make it—would have turned one. Or two. Or three. Or fourteen. Or twenty. Or thirty-five. This is the day she would have spent with family, blowing out candles. Eating cake. Celebrating with loved ones. Opening gifts. But she's not here. And you're questioning Me all over again: Why did I take her from you? What did you do wrong? How could you have changed things? How different—how much sweeter—would your life have been if I hadn't robbed you of this child? Oh, My sweet daughter, how I long to bring comfort, especially on days like today. I didn't come to steal, kill, or destroy. That is the work of the enemy. I came to bring life—and abundant life at that! I long to wrap My arms of comfort around you and remind you, even on the hardest of days, that I am the Author of life. As you shed a few tears today, remember that joy comes in the morning. And sometimes, even though it's hard to see, joy also comes in the mourning.

LOSS OF PEACE

. . . .

*You will keep in perfect peace those whose minds
are steadfast, because they trust in you.*

ISAIAH 26:3 NIV

You're not happy with life as you now know it. You wish things were different. Why can't you have the blissful, carefree life that so many of your friends and coworkers have? Wouldn't that be lovely? It hardly seems fair. The turmoil you face on a daily basis—some of it brought on by others, some by your situation—is wearing you down. If only you could go back to a peaceful, untroubled place where anxiety didn't rule the day. Then things would be different. You'd be a better person, one who didn't fret over every little thing. But you can't go back. Neither can you seem to move forward. You're stuck right here with your feet in quicksand. Oh, sweet daughter, you don't have to wait until things are different to be at peace. Don't grieve where you're at. Take a deep breath and begin to praise Me in the very middle of the anxiety. I love to see you overwhelmed—not by circumstances—but by a supernatural peace that passes understanding. Remain steadfast. Put your trust in Me, and I promise I will keep you in perfect peace, no matter the situation.

FAILED GOALS

*I press on toward the goal for the prize of the
upward call of God in Christ Jesus.*

PHILIPPIANS 3:14 ESV

You are not a failure. Listen to those words again, My
child. You may have failed at what you were attempt-
ing—in fact, you might have failed multiple times in a
row—but that does not make you a failure. Maybe you
overshot a little. Maybe you didn't hit the mark. You
ended up disappointed. But that's okay. At least you gave
it a great amount of effort, as always. I love watching you
try. . .and try. . .and try again. I appreciate your tenacity.
I enjoy your persistence. You've never been one to give
up, no matter how high the obstacle. So go ahead and set
those goals. Shoot for the stars. Aim as high as you can.
But don't depend fully on yourself as you aim toward the
mark. Let Me be the wind that pushes you. Let Me be the
vision caster. And let Me be the One who scoops you into
My arms when you stumble and fall. You are amazing, My
child! Together, we'll do great things. Let's aim for that
next goal, hand in hand.

Choosing the Other Parent

*The LORD is close to the brokenhearted and
saves those who are crushed in spirit.*

PSALM 34:18 NIV

Your child has chosen to live with someone else, and it's
breaking your heart. You're confused. This decision makes
no sense at all. It's a slap in the face, a hit to the gut. After
all you've done to pour yourself out. . .now this? You're
wondering what you could have done differently. You're
angry at the other adult, wishing he would support you.
More than anything, you miss the child who's moved on.
You genuinely wish things were better between you. You
feel helpless and just want life to go back to normal. But
how can it? There's a rift that needs healing. I understand
broken relationships. I know the agony of having a child
choose someone—or something—over Me. What a sting!
But I also know what it is to watch that same child repent
and turn her heart back toward home. So give this situation
time. Give your child space. Trust that I can and will use
time to do a very special (and likely unexpected) work in
your child's heart. Can you trust Me, daughter? Then look
forward to better days ahead.

The Next Shoe

Search me, God, and know my heart;
test me and know my anxious thoughts.

PSALM 139:23 NIV

You've lived through tragedy after tragedy, and it seems
to be coming in a stream. You're afraid to close your eyes,
to take a breath, because you're wondering when the next
shoe will drop. None of this seems fair or right. Why have
you been selected for so much pain? You raise your fist to
Me and shake it in anger, crying, "Don't You care, God?"
The grief is causing your knees to buckle and your faith
to waver. Worry has long since replaced hope. Instead of
waking up wondering what amazing things the day will
hold, you wake up wondering what tragedy awaits. Oh,
sweet daughter, I do see, and I care more than you know.
I'm not a cruel Father, hovering over you to drop one tragedy after another. My heart breaks every time yours does.
This fallen world you live in came about as a result of sin.
It wasn't My doing. And all the pain you've experienced is
a direct result of that sin as well. No, I am not out to hurt
you. I'm here to love you, to show you that you can and
will make it through. So don't run away. Run toward Me,
and let Me help you through this tough season.

LOSS OF ABILITY

Yet this I call to mind and therefore I have hope: Because of the LORD's great love we are not consumed, for his compassions never fail. They are new every morning; great is your faithfulness.

Ability. It's a fascinating word, one you know well. I see you, working in your own ability to try to make things happen. I also see when you're unable to press your way through to success. Hard as you may try, nothing seems to be coming together lately. It doesn't make sense to you. You're a go-getter. You make things happen. Why not now? Why not here? In the secret hours of the night you wonder if this is going to be a forever problem. Maybe you've lost your touch. Perhaps you'll never get it back again. Don't worry! These seasons of "inability" provide you the perfect opportunity to test My ability to perform on your behalf. Watch and see if I won't open the windows of heaven and prove that all ability comes from above. You've been a lovely conduit, but sometimes I like to work alone. So sit back and watch Me take over. You might just get a kick out of what's coming next.

LACK OF INTIMACY
WITH CLOSE FRIENDS

· ·

But the fruit of the Spirit is love, joy, peace,
patience, kindness, goodness, faithfulness,
gentleness, self-control; against such
things there is no law.

GALATIANS 5:22–23 ESV

You were created for closeness—with Me, and with others. And now you're in a season where distance seems to be growing between you and those friends you've held dear. You used to have lunch together. You went to the mall. You had coffee. Your children had playdates. You laughed over silly things and swapped stories about marriage and parenting. Now those friendships appear to be waning. Life, in its overwhelming way, has prevented the usual get-togethers or phone calls. You're grieving that fact. You're even wondering if you've done something to cause the separation. Don't people want to hang out with you anymore? Can't they carve out a little time for you? I promise that intimate friendships lie ahead. I've got plenty of children whose heartbeats are in sync with yours. They need you as much as you need them. Some you haven't even met yet. Others you already know but haven't connected with on a personal level. Let this season pass, and then watch out! You'll be busier than ever, building friendships and enjoying those I place in your path.

THERE'S COMING A DAY

Dear friends, now we are children of God, and what we will be has not yet been made known. But we know that when Christ appears, we shall be like him, for we shall see him as he is.

1 JOHN 3:2 NIV

There's coming a day when all will be revealed. Things that haven't made sense—sin, sickness, pain, and agony—will be no more. Grief will be washed away, a thing of the past. When I appear (and I'm coming again on clouds of glory), every tear will be wiped away. Anguish will cease. Broken bodies will be completely and totally mended with no pain whatsoever. On that day, you will see clearer than you ever have that you were—and are—created in My image. You're not just My child; you're like Me in more ways than you could have fathomed. In eternity there will be no heavy weights. There will be no sorrow. Eternity's promise is not a fanciful notion. It's very, very real. Until we reach that point where all things are made new again, will you trust Me to move on your behalf? Though things aren't perfect in the here and now, there's coming a day when they will be. And when that day comes, all your sorrows will be long forgotten.

Those Questions

. . . .

Therefore there is now no condemnation for those who are in Christ Jesus. For the law of the Spirit of life in Christ Jesus has set you free from the law of sin and of death. For what the Law could not do, weak as it was through the flesh, God did: sending His own Son in the likeness of sinful flesh and as an offering for sin, He condemned sin in the flesh.

ROMANS 8:1–3 NASB

I hear those questions going through your mind. You've been through a shaking, something akin to an emotional earthquake. It has left you reeling. You're wondering if you did enough. You're questioning every little thing, replaying the scenarios in your head. Oh, how I wish you could let go of the unnecessary guilt you're feeling. There is no condemnation in Me. None whatsoever. You're human. You didn't get every little detail right, perhaps. But that doesn't mean you loved less, cared less, or worked less. I'm proud of your efforts. Truly proud. The only questions you need to ask right now are "How can I move forward from here?" and "Lord, will You be my guide?" I will nudge you forward. Give you direction at each turn in the road. And I'm going to be here every step of the way to keep your thoughts focused on where they should be, not on the regrets of yesterday.

BEAUTIFUL SCARS

From now on let no one cause me trouble,
for I bear on my body the marks of Jesus.

GALATIANS 6:17 ESV

Some of the wounds you've suffered in this life have left you with deep emotional scars. Oh, how you would like to cover them up, to pretend they don't exist. To your way of thinking, those scars have made you ugly, but nothing could be further from the truth. Those scars are beautiful in My eyes. They stand as a testament to the things we have endured together. Every one has healed up stronger than before and stands as a testament to My promise to heal you from the inside out. You are victorious. You're an overcomer. You've been through things that would have caused others to crumble. Yet here you are, still standing, still moving forward. Perhaps you think no one understands, but I do. I endured several scars Myself. That day on the cross My hands, feet, and side were wounded. I took the stripes upon My back as well. Why? So that you could be healed. The next time you look at the emotional scars from what you've been through, remember. . .I understand, and I see you as healed and whole.

Nurturing Yourself

Surely goodness and mercy shall follow me
all the days of my life, and I shall dwell
in the house of the LORD forever.

PSALM 23:6 ESV

I designed your body, heart, and mind to transition from one stage of life to another. If you've been paying attention (and I know you have), you realize that the transitions between those various stages are usually tougher than you thought they would be. Women are born nurturers. I designed you to care for others, whether you have children or not. In your later years you transition to caregiver for aging parents. Your body, thoughts, and heart issues are ever changing, and that's how you were meant to be. Because you spend so many years helping and caring for others, you often forget to take care of yourself. It's time to rediscover your own individual passions and goals. I'm here to help you with that. Let's start by shifting your perspective. For once, I'm going to ask you to focus on yourself and not the ones around you. Yes, *you.* What are you hoping for over these next few years? What desires are motivating you? Let's rediscover those passions together and move into the next great adventure.

LOSS OF A JOB

. . . .

"Have I not commanded you? Be strong and
courageous. Do not be afraid; do not be
discouraged, for the LORD your God
will be with you wherever you go."

JOSHUA 1:9 NIV

I see what's going on in that heart of yours, My child. This
job loss makes you feel as though you have no value. No
importance. You wonder if you will find a place to fit in
again or a way to contribute. You're pondering the financial
issues and wishing you had a way to bring in money with
a job you really love. Does such a job exist? If so, will you
find it? Will a new company treat you with respect? Rest
easy, My child. I haven't forgotten you. It's time to pull
out that résumé and show 'em what you've got. You are
valuable, you know. In fact, you're an amazing employee.
And you will find a place to settle in, a wonderful new
place with opportunities you've not yet had. With that
in mind, I hope you will begin to see this job loss in perspective. You're a hop, skip, and jump away from where
I'm taking you. Don't spend any time looking back. We
have a wonderful road ahead of us, after all.

LOSS OF CONFIDENCE

*So do not throw away your confidence;
it will be richly rewarded.*

HEBREWS 10:35 NIV

I see your sagging shoulders. I know when your confidence is waning. It's written all over your face. You're ready to give up. Want to know something? It only happens when you take your eyes off Me and put them on yourself. I never created you to be overly confident in yourself, after all. It's your confidence in Me that causes you to square your shoulders, look your problems in the eye, and know—without a shadow of a doubt—that today's troubles will work out for your good. Check out what My Word has to say on the subject. Don't throw away your confidence. Don't toss it in the nearest trash can or hide it under the covers. Don't curl up in a ball in the corner. Not now. Just put your confidence in Me. In other words, shift your focus. This is the time to lift eyes, heart, and head. I'm a rewarder of perfectly aimed confidence. It gives Me great pleasure to watch you transition from terrified to triumphant. So let's go! I'm about to give you an injection of confidence that will boost your courage and set you on the right path.

LOSS OF MEMORY

I remember the days of old; I meditate on all that you have done; I ponder the work of your hands.

PSALM 143:5 ESV

Oh, those memories. They are sweet. . .often bittersweet. And now they seem to be fading. The things that used to come easily? Not quite as easily now. You try. I see you trying. But something is amiss. You're not able to recall, to remember. Will all your yesterdays dissolve into a giant blur? This change is making you anxious, worried. You're wondering if you'll make it through this season and still maintain your ability to function on your own. Should you tell others that your memory is leaving? Will they figure it out on their own? Will they look down on you? Will they offer to help? How will you humble yourself to accept help, if they offer? I hear these questions running through your heart, and I have answers. I have people in mind to help during this season. They will gather around you and make sure you have what you need. And I'll be there, too. I love you so dearly, and I promise I will never leave you or forsake you. The very best memories are ahead, dear one. You. Me. Together. We'll get through this.

LOSING YOUR WAY

Let love and faithfulness never leave you;
bind them around your neck,
write them on the tablet of your heart.

PROVERBS 3:3 NIV

You used to have 20/20 vision. I can remember times when you were so in tune to My Spirit that guiding you from here to there came easy. Lately, however, your emotions have been in a whirlwind. It's getting harder and harder for you to find your bearings or to hear My voice. At times you feel like you're in a forest, surrounded by towering trees. You can't see past them. You can't maneuver around them. There's no clear path laid out to guide your feet. I've been paying close attention, and I see that you're feeling ungrounded in this unfamiliar territory. You aren't sure where you are or what's coming next. Fear grips you at times, and you're frozen in place. I just want to remind you that I'm right here, and I'm rock solid. I'm not moving. I'm not changing. I'm not going to disappear on you, no matter what things "feel" like. With one word I can clear the trees from the forest. With a breath I can create a path, clearly visible. All you have to do is look to Me. Speak in faith. Trust Me to do the rest. You'll never be lost as long as I'm your guide.

Moving Down the Totem Pole

For You formed my inward parts; You wove me in my mother's womb. I will give thanks to You, for I am fearfully and wonderfully made; wonderful are Your works, and my soul knows it very well.

PSALM 139:13–14 NASB

I see the value that My children put in status. You work, work, work your way up the ladder and then grieve when you begin to slip back down again. What a hard life it must be, battling to be on top. And how difficult to always be in competition with your peers. I don't want this for you. No more scrambling to be the top dog. I want you to rest easy, child. No striving. I'll get you to where you need to go. That's a promise. You can take it to the bank. And I won't hurt anyone else in the process. (How's that for going against the flow?) My plan doesn't involve racing against the clock. There's no pressure to prove yourself better than the next guy. Just be you. . . the you I created you to be. I've known from day one, the very moment you were conceived, in fact, what you would be when you grew up. Never once did I plan for you to fret about your status along the way. The totem pole? In My plan, it doesn't even exist.

That Teenager

Your children are growing up. This has been quite the adventure for you. I see that. But there are times—like now—when you grieve the growing. As your little ones transition into teens, the changes can be tough. There are emotional outbursts, clothing arguments, messy bedrooms, piles of laundry, school woes, peer pressure, and a host of other challenges guaranteed to make even the strongest parent want to pull her hair out. How will you make the journey down this bumpy road? With My Word, of course. I've given you everything you need to guide your children through their teenage years. It's all right there in the Bible. My words are useful for teaching, for correcting, and for training. That's what you are, you know—a personal trainer. And by the way, you're doing a fine job, so stop fretting. Don't grieve this season too much. It'll be over in the blink of an eye, after all. We'll plow through together. Grab your Bible and let's get going.

LACK OF INTIMACY WITH SPOUSE

*Though one may be overpowered,
two can defend themselves. A cord of
three strands is not quickly broken.*

ECCLESIASTES 4:12 NIV

You're feeling neglected by the one who's supposed to love you most—your spouse. Your times of intimacy are waning. The spark that once lit your private times is threatening to go out. You often wonder if he will ever look at you as he once did or if your days of romantic interludes are behind you. A thousand questions roll through your mind. You blame yourself. You blame him. You blame Me. But you're not giving up. You've tried any number of things to woo him back to that place of intimacy, but he's too busy, too tired. And when he's not. . . you are. What a difficult time this is. Oh, but I can add the necessary spark. I can do (in the supernatural) what cannot be done in the natural. Give this situation to Me. I can soften hearts, transform thought patterns, and stir up feelings that might have died long ago. In the natural, these things would be impossible. But I'm a God of the supernatural. Watch as I go above and beyond to reignite this flickering flame.

FLABBERGASTED

"Be still, and know that I am God.
I will be exalted among the nations,
I will be exalted in the earth!"

PSALM 46:10 ESV

There's been a shaking, and it's got you completely rattled. A rift in a friendship has hit you out of nowhere and knocked the breath out of you. What started as a misunderstanding has morphed into a full-out war. Words have flown back and forth. Tempers are raging. You don't understand how things got to this point. You can't seem to fix it, though you've tried valiantly. You're left feeling dejected, frustrated, betrayed, bewildered, and flabbergasted. You're also battling feelings of loneliness, now that one who has been such an important part of your life is no longer in the picture. I understand these feelings of betrayal. I've had once-close friends turn their backs on Me for no apparent reason. I've had friends turn away because of a misunderstanding. I've loved them anyway and done My best to woo them back. But not everyone comes back. Not every relationship is healed. It takes two willing parties to develop a friendship, after all. Don't give up, though. Keep praying, keep trying, and keep that door open, at least for now. Most of all, don't panic. Just because you're struggling with one friend doesn't mean you're destined to lose all of them. Rest easy. I'll take it from here.

A WORLD OF GRAY

. . . .

The LORD is close to the brokenhearted
and saves those who are crushed in spirit.

PSALM 34:18 NIV

Grief has changed you. It has affected your vision, both literal and figurative. Those who love you and care about your well-being are concerned. They've tried to intervene, but you just can't shake what you're feeling. A once-bright world has faded to gray—bland, colorless. Nothing looks or sounds the same when encased in dense, dismal fog. Colors that once popped have dulled to neutral. Every sound is muffled, muted. Foods you once loved are now bland and flavorless. A cloud hovers over you. It seems to follow you wherever you go. You've learned to prefer the cloud, haven't you? When it lifts for moments of brief sunlight, the waves of grief come. They rock you to the core. You're swept back in time. A special anniversary. A birthday. A photograph. These things take hold, and you dive back under the cloud again to ride out the emotions. Oh, how I want to see you walking in the sunlight again. Will you trust Me to lead you there? I long to free you from the cloud, once and for all, if you will let Me. I'm skilled at cloud lifting, so watch as I reveal blue skies. Before long, you'll be walking in the sunlight once again.

A Change in View

*By wisdom a house is built, and through
understanding it is established;
through knowledge its rooms are filled
with rare and beautiful treasures.*

PROVERBS 24:3–4 NIV

Things aren't the same in your new home, are they? The scenery isn't the same. The view out of the window isn't the same. The layout of the house isn't the same. You long for the old days, when a drive through the neighborhood brought a sensation of comfort and feelings of home. Now you just feel lost. The terrain seems pale in comparison. You haven't "owned" the neighborhood yet. In short, you're feeling a little homesick for the old place. I understand homesickness, trust Me. I left My home in heaven to come to earth for over thirty-three years. It would be an understatement to say that things weren't the same. Nothing looked or felt like what I was accustomed to. But I was willing to make the move so that I could perform the ultimate act of love: die on the cross for you. Don't grieve this move. You will adjust. Before long, this place will be comfortable. You will feel settled, whole. If you need any motivation in the meantime, just open My Word and read My story. Perhaps you'll learn a few things to apply to your own journey as you make this new house your home.

FEELING LEFT OUT

. . . .

" 'But I will restore you to health and heal your wounds,' " declares the LORD, " 'because you are called an outcast, Zion for whom no one cares.' "

JEREMIAH 30:17 NIV

I see your broken heart. You feel left out. They didn't include you in their plans again. They didn't invite you to their event. They haven't included you as you've wished they would for some time now. It seems unfair. Everyone else has a role to play. . .except you. You feel like an outsider, on the fringes, while everyone else has the time of their lives. Seems like only yesterday you were one of them, always at the center of the action. Now everything's flipped upside down, inside out. They're part of the group and you're not. Why don't they seem to want you around? Why don't you get the invitations like the others? Why has so much distance grown, causing a chasm? What can you do to bridge the gap? These are all familiar questions. I experienced something similar Myself. I was rejected—a Man of Sorrows, acquainted with grief. Friends turned their backs on Me. People I loved let Me down. They walked away from Me. But I learned, in the solitude, how to draw near to My Father and let Him be the One who mattered most. That's My desire for you, too. Draw near. You'll learn all you need to know about friendship as you put your hand in the hand of the One who created you. He'll be your best friend ever.

Loss of a Grown Child

*Then Jacob tore his clothes, put on sackcloth and
mourned for his son many days. All his sons
and daughters came to comfort him, but he refused
to be comforted. "No," he said, "I will continue
to mourn until I join my son in the grave."
So his father wept for him.*

GENESIS 37:34–35 NIV

My heart aches alongside those who have lost a child at
any age. But oh, the pain of losing one you've loved and
nurtured for so many precious years. Losing a grown child
is heartbreaking. I see that you're questioning yourself. You
wonder if you could have done more. Oh, My daughter,
you did a fabulous job raising that child. You did your very
best. I see that you want the time back. It seemed to fly.
You long for things past; you grieve the times that will be
no more. You yearn for do-overs and wish you could clean
up some messes. There's no need for any do-overs. There
are no messes to clean. It's time now to focus on the good
times you had together—the trips you took, the antics
of that child as a youngster, school programs. . . These are
the things I want you to remember. Think on the many
times your child made you laugh, made you sigh, and
made your heart sing. More joyous days are ahead when
you see your loved one in heaven. Until then, do your best
to focus on the sweetness, not the pain.

The Photograph

. . . .

In the day of my trouble I seek the Lord;
in the night my hand is stretched out without
wearying; my soul refuses to be comforted.

PSALM 77:2 ESV

You're looking at his picture. That handsome face. That strong physique. His winning smile. As you hold the photo in your hands, the pain in your heart is magnified. You see in that familiar, loving face the pain of what you've lost. How could someone so healthy, so strong, be gone? Oh, but look closer, My child. See what I see—a life well lived. A person of great worth who graced your life with laughter, conversation, love, and warmth. Let that sink in. The photo you're holding in your hand is a reminder of the great blessing your loved one was to so many. Wasn't he one of the greatest people to ever walk the face of the earth? Didn't he bless people everywhere he went? Weren't you fortunate to have him in your life? Your loved one was My gift to many. And now, as you reflect on all of his goodness, it's time to look at his many good traits in perspective. Take them on yourself. Become the person he would want you to be. This will be your gift back to him and to the many people you have yet to bless in your own life.

LOSS OF PASSION FOR GOD

*Whom have I in heaven but you? And there is
nothing on earth that I desire besides you.
My flesh and my heart may fail, but God is
the strength of my heart and my portion forever.*

PSALM 73:25–26 ESV

I know you sense it. Your passion for Me—your zeal for
our quiet times—is waning. Instead of rushing into the
throne room each morning, you check your e-mail. You
sign onto social media. You text a friend or a loved one.
It didn't used to be this way. You would awake with a
song of praise on your lips and a desire for togetherness.
Whatever happened to those days when you began the
morning in My presence? Remember those times when
you rushed My way, dove into My Word, and poured out
your heart? What great times we had. It's not too late to
reignite that passion. With just a word from you, I will
run your way. I will stir you to action. I'll take you past
the grief, pain, and other issues that have separated us. So
lift your eyes and heart. Let Me tear down those carefully
placed walls you've put up. Draw close and watch as the
flame is relit. No, things won't be like they once were.
They will be even better.

A Big Anniversary

*I think it is right to refresh your memory
as long as I live in the tent of this body.*

2 PETER 1:13 NIV

It's been years since you lost your loved one. Most days the memories don't haunt you like they used to. But a big anniversary is coming up. You're dreading it. Other thoughts have been consuming you of late as well. I know, because I see those thoughts; I hear those heart-cries. You're reaching the point in the grieving process where your thoughts are shifting. Your memories bring with them sweeping feelings of gratitude and joy. How blessed you were to have this amazing person in your life. What a blessing to have the time you did. And now, as you reflect, you've made up your mind not to give in to despair. I love that about you. Your loved one wouldn't want that for you. She saw value in you. She saw strength, no matter how deeply buried. She nurtured those things and caused them to grow. More than anything, she would be proud of the person you have become and how you've honored her memory. I'm proud, too. You're walking in My strength daily, and that brings Me joy.

GETTING OVERLOOKED

*"Do not let your hearts be troubled.
You believe in God; believe also in me."*

JOHN 14:1 NIV

You feel overlooked. Left out. You wonder if anyone notices you or even pays attention to all the hard work you do. Sometimes you feel like your acts of service are counterproductive because no one even seems to realize the hours you're putting in. They don't thank you. They don't seem to care. They take you for granted. I understand these feelings, trust Me. I often feel overlooked Myself. I do so much for My children, and they often forget to thank Me or acknowledge what I've done on their behalf. It's a knife to the heart, isn't it? But don't spend too much time fretting over what others do (or don't do). Don't let your heart be troubled. Instead, spend as much time as you can in My presence. I'll put it all into perspective for you. I promise. You'll be stronger from the inside out if you shift your gaze from those who've overlooked you to the One who never will. Give that broken heart to Me, and watch as I craft you into an amazing woman of God who will always include others.

Separation by War

- -

"Because he holds fast to me in love,
I will deliver him; I will protect him,
because he knows my name."

PSALM 91:14 ESV

Someone you love has left—not just the city or the state, but the country. He's headed off to serve his country, and you're at a loss to know how to respond. How do you pray? How do you get back to normal daily life? Should you link arms with other military spouses? Should you stay busy so that you don't go crazy while the one you love is away? Should you dive into your work and do your best to forget about the pain until you are reunited once again? I have a great suggestion: hold tight to Me with one hand and use the other to grab hold of those who are still nearby. They are struggling, too. You're a team and can get through this together. Keep pressing forward. It might feel like your feet are slogging through the sand right now, but those feelings will pass. Keep shuffling. If you begin to move in reverse, I'll change your course. The point is to keep your eyes on the goal. And remember, this season will come to an end. It will. It seems eternal now, but it's not. Before long, you'll be celebrating the homecoming of your loved one.

DESPAIR

* *

*But we have this treasure in earthen vessels,
so that the surpassing greatness of the power
will be of God and not from ourselves; we are
afflicted in every way, but not crushed; perplexed,
but not despairing; persecuted, but not forsaken;
struck down, but not destroyed; always carrying
about in the body the dying of Jesus, so that the
life of Jesus also may be manifested in our body.*

2 CORINTHIANS 4:7–10 NASB

Despair. What an intense and complicated word. To despair means that you've completely lost hope. You're at a total loss to know what to do. You can't dig your way out, nor do you care. Oh, My child. . .what a difficult place to set up camp. What a hard place to be. My children reach the point of despair when they completely lose sight of Me and doubt My ability (or My willingness) to intervene on their behalf while in crisis. It's hard to picture at this very moment, but I haven't forgotten you. I'm still God even in the midst of the turmoil and pain. And though you may think you're unreachable, nothing could be further from the truth. Nothing is beyond My power to remedy or redeem. Don't make up your mind to drive those stakes even farther into the ground. Allow Me to yank them up, once and for all. Let's face this despair together and watch the dark clouds lift.

DISABILITY

· ·

*Behold, what manner of love the Father hath
bestowed upon us, that we should be called
the sons of God: therefore the world knoweth
us not, because it knew him not.*

1 JOHN 3:1 KJV

You often look at yourself as flawed, don't you? I see those thoughts churning through your head. You take what others have labeled a disability, a flaw, an imperfection, and have judged yourself too harshly, which has greatly limited the possibilities of where you can go and what you can become. You've grieved this perceived loss, but I don't look at things that way at all! I see you as someone who is specially-abled! You've been gifted with an intuitive God-sense that causes you to do more, not less! Instead of looking ahead and fearing the what-ifs, turn your gaze to Me and watch as I supernaturally empower you to go above and beyond all expectations. Don't let anyone—or anything—limit you. Do you think for one moment that My plan for your life is any less than the plan I have for someone else? You are dearly loved. You are My child. I've got amazing things planned for your future. Look ahead! The road is bright and filled with amazing adventures. That's a promise!

INFERTILITY

. . . .

For it is written: "Be glad, barren woman,
you who never bore a child; shout for joy
and cry aloud, you who were never in labor;
because more are the children of the desolate
woman than of her who has a husband."

Longing. Aching. Praying. Begging. I see what you're going through. I hear your cries. You ache for a child. You won't give up until you have one in your arms. I understand totally. I created you to nurture, to love. Right now you feel as though you have a thorn in your side. You cringe every time you see a post on social media about a friend or loved one who's expecting. You crawl deeper into the hole of depression as you visit a friend who's nursing her newborn. You wonder if I will ever come through for you as I have for them. Oh, how I long to encourage you today! Look at the story of Hannah in 1 Samuel. For years she prayed for a child. She dedicated that child to Me, long before he (Samuel) was born. She never gave up, no matter how bleak the picture looked. There's something to be said for that kind of tenacity. My heart is moved by people who don't give up. It's time to begin speaking words of dedication over the child you don't yet have. Make a pledge to raise that little one in My love, My care. In other words, speak life into your situation. I'm a life-giving God, after all! I can't wait to show you what the future holds.

A TRUSTING SEASON

*"But seek first the kingdom of God
and his righteousness, and all these
things will be added to you."*

MATTHEW 6:33 ESV

It doesn't matter how long you've worked for a particular company; losing your job can be a kick to the gut. Why did they let you go? Don't they realize how desperately you need that job, that income? After all the years you've poured yourself out on their behalf, it feels like a betrayal. I see the financial fears you're wrestling with. I sense the worries about the future. How will you pay your utility bills? Your rent? Your car payment? It's impossible with no income. You're also concerned about your coworkers. You'll miss them. You'll miss the family environment. My sweet child, this is a trusting season, for sure! (Do you trust Me? Then, hang tight!) It might seem impossible to believe that I have something bigger and better in mind for you, but that's how I work. Before long, this job loss will be a distant memory. You'll be safely tucked away into that new job, meeting new people, earning a good living, and taking care of your bills on time. Don't give up now. Trust Me in the trusting season.

LOSS OF A SIBLING

. . . .

*For I consider that the sufferings of this present
time are not worth comparing with the
glory that is to be revealed to us.*

ROMANS 8:18 ESV

I created you to live in a family, and you've been a delight to those around you. How you've loved them! You're a natural with people. But now you're grieving the loss of one you held dear, a sibling. Your heart is broken, and you wonder if you're dreaming. Maybe you'll wake up and she'll still be there after all. Perhaps you'll pinch yourself and discover it was just a bad dream, a horrifying nightmare. Your mind reels back in time to your childhood. How many precious memories you shared! Camping adventures. Summer pool parties. School bus adventures. And now those memories bring a mixture of pain and joy. My heart goes out to you. I want you to know how much your sibling loved you. Sure, there were times of squabbling, but love runs deeper than all that. And don't forget—you'll reconnect in the blink of an eye. Heaven will be filled with amazing adventures, far beyond what you experienced as a child. So draw a deep breath. Let the memories come. But don't grieve for long, because you will be reunited in the great by and by.

BURSTS OF ANGER

"In your anger do not sin": Do not let the sun go down while you are still angry.

EPHESIANS 4:26 NIV

You're angry at Me. I understand. You blame Me. You wonder why I didn't step in and do something. *What kind of God would allow something so terrible to happen? Why didn't You rush to save? Can You be trusted with the next tragedy?* I hear your cries in the night, sweet daughter, and I see the broken places in your heart where anger and grief escape like oil from a broken well. Agony displays itself in strange ways, and anger is just one of the many I've witnessed in the lives of My children. It's okay to be mad. Go ahead and cry out to the heavens. Ask your "Why?" questions. But please remember that you live in a world that was broken by sin. I never created My kids to experience the kind of pain you've been through. I had in mind a much kinder place. Also remember that heaven is just around the bend. There will be no tears there. Anger, too, will be a thing of the past. You won't be asking any hard questions in heaven, either. You'll be far too busy praising and worshipping to ponder the griefs of the past. Lift your eyes, sweet one. Rest that heart. Release that anger and be healed.

LOSS OF IDENTITY

. . . .

Do not love the world or anything in the world.
If anyone loves the world, love for the Father
is not in them. For everything in the world—the
lust of the flesh, the lust of the eyes, and the pride
of life—comes not from the Father but from the
world. The world and its desires pass away,
but whoever does the will of God lives forever.

1 JOHN 2:15–17 NIV

Time marches like a drummer in a band, the rhythm never ending. You grow. You change. And these changes are holy. I've created you to change, to morph and adjust to life as it moves forward. This is especially true after you've lost a loved one. You've spent your whole life focusing on that loved one, after all. You've catered to his needs. You've worked to show how much he was loved. Now he's not here and you're not needed in the same way. This forces you into an adjustment phase. Oh, I see what you're really struggling with, My child: This is a loss of identity. You're not sure who you are without this person. You're not just grieving; you're at a loss to know what to do with yourself. You need to be needed. Remember, your identity isn't in what you do or even whom you do it for. Your identity is in Me. If you'll keep that in the forefront of your mind, you will have an easier time adjusting to the road ahead.

Loss of a Foster Child

I brought a special little one into your life. You cared for that precious child much longer than you'd expected. Her joyous smile rooted itself in your heart. The attachment grew over time, and you dreaded the day she would return to her own family. Now that day is here, and you're heartbroken. How can you give up this sweet one now when the bond is stronger than ever? I'm right here to help you through this transition. Remember, I'm going with this child. She's not going to be alone, even though you won't be with her. I have an amazing plan for her life. Oh, how I wish I could show you! The role you've played has been foundational, critical. You'll never know the impact you've made in her life. I'm so very proud of you for taking in one of My little ones and giving her this glorious opportunity in a safe place. Now trust Me as I lead her where she needs to go.

MISCARRIAGE

*The LORD is close to the brokenhearted
and saves those who are crushed in spirit.*

PSALM 34:18 NIV

Oh, dear one! I see that heart—shattered, crushed, split in two. I understand every thought going through your mind. Why did I let this happen? Do I not care? Did I not see? Could I not have stopped it? You desperately longed for a child. The good news came. . .and then that child was ripped from your womb. You're sickened inside. How do you shift from thrilled to horrified in such a short period of time? Why wasn't this particular baby given a chance at life? Why would I allow this to happen? Sweet daughter, My heart is broken alongside yours. I love this baby. In fact, I'm right here, gazing into that sweet face even now. And while you won't see her in your lifetime, you will see her in eternity. She'll be waiting for you. . .I promise. In the meantime, she's in perfect health, playing, romping, enjoying all that heaven has to offer. One day you will, too. Until then, I will do everything I can to strengthen you and see you through what seems like an impossible season.

Clothed in Grief

. . . .

*Be merciful to me, LORD, for I am
in distress; my eyes grow weak with sorrow,
my soul and body with grief.*

PSALM 31:9 NIV

I see that blanket you're wearing. It's wrapped tight around you, cutting off your oxygen. That hot, cumbersome blanket—half friend, half foe—has become your ally and your worst enemy. As much as you'd love to toss it, it's become a part of you. Your identity is wound up in its fibers. Grieving can be a good thing, up to a point. Emotions are raw and real and must be given their proper place to bring ultimate cleansing. But My hope, My desire for you during this critical season is that you don't allow it to become your identity. Don't let it suffocate you. Don't let it stifle you. Don't let it rob you of relationships with those you love. A day is coming, and it might not be long from now, when I'm going to help you peel off that outer garment you're clinging to. When that day comes, you'll be able to breathe again, to walk freely once more. So brace yourself. Get ready to trust Me to do the work that I long to do. Together, we'll toss that old cloak of grief and put on a colorful garment of praise.

An Empty Womb

*So we fix our eyes not on what is seen,
but on what is unseen, since what is seen is
temporary, but what is unseen is eternal.*

2 Corinthians 4:18 niv

It makes no sense. People who don't even want (or to your way of thinking, *need*) children are pregnant. And you? Your womb is empty. Despite all attempts, it hasn't happened for you. And now you're losing hope. You're angry. That anger is beginning to show in multiple areas of your life. The empty spaces are quickly filling with bitterness and judgment against those who hold children in their arms. Oh, My sweet daughter, take a deep breath. I make all things beautiful in My time. And though it makes no sense at all right now, I have wonderful plans for your little family. So don't give up hope. Don't let envy or bitterness consume you while you're waiting. Keep speaking life to that womb. Keep gazing upward at Me instead of at those around you. One day your disappointment will fade away, replaced by fulfillment and joy. I see that "mama heart" inside of you, and I will fill it in My way and My time.

FORECLOSURE

. . . .

"Peace I leave with you; my peace I give you. I do not give to you as the world gives. Do not let your hearts be troubled and do not be afraid."

JOHN 14:27 NIV

The impossible has happened. That home you've loved, the one you chose specifically for your family, has been lost to foreclosure. You watched with a sick feeling in your gut as all attempts to keep it failed. Gone are the carpets and hardwood floors you picked out. Gone are the kitchen cabinets you selected. Gone are the walls you painted. Those things that meant so much to you aren't yours anymore. Gone is all the money that you poured into the place to turn it from a house to a home. My heart aches with you at this loss. I know how uprooted you feel right now, how lost and brokenhearted. Please don't agonize for long. There will be another home to love. There will be a place to put down roots. It won't look the same. It won't have the same colors, the same floors. But it will feel like home because those you love will be there with you. Trust Me during the interim, child. It's a hard transition, but we will make it through together. . .I promise.

LOSS OF STATUS

*So my heart began to despair over
all my toilsome labor under the sun.*

ECCLESIASTES 2:20 NIV

Some call it status. You've experienced it, felt the joy of moving up the ladder, and now you feel it's slipped away. You're confused. You feel like you're losing your footing. All your attempts to rectify the situation have failed. . . and you feel like a failure. How can a person go from the top rung to the bottom in such a short period of time? You're humiliated and have no answers when people ask you what has happened. I understand the loss of status. After all, I left a throne in heaven to come to earth. I took on human flesh—with all of its temptations and pains— to accomplish the greatest act of all time. And though it might have appeared to others that I had lost everything, I'd really gained the whole world. Perhaps that's what's happening to you right now, too. If you pause to think about the work I'm accomplishing in your heart, you will see that I have even greater things for you to accomplish during this season of your life. Hang on! Good things are around the bend. And please don't obsess over what others might be thinking. The only opinion that matters right now is Mine, and I'm convinced you're terrific.

LOSS OF NEIGHBORS

For though I am absent in body, yet I am with you in spirit, rejoicing to see your good order and the firmness of your faith in Christ.

COLOSSIANS 2:5 ESV

I understand your need for companionship. Having people nearby that you can depend on is a great gift. I know you're feeling a loss since your neighbors moved away. Things just won't be the same, will they? I just want to remind you that I am still here, and I'm the very best friend of all. No matter who moves into that empty house, I will still be the One who longs to spend quality time with you, to swap stories, to inspire your family, to join with you in fun projects. I want to be the One who helps you figure out the hard answers to life's most difficult questions. In short, I want to be more than just a neighbor; I want to be your very best friend. If you need Me, just call and I'll show up in a hurry. And here's another bit of good news: I'll never move away. I'm not going anywhere. You'll never see a SOLD sign in My yard. There will be no empty house to stare at. I'm staying put, right here in the neighborhood. And I'll be the best neighbor you've ever had.

Broken Relationship
with a Friend

. . . .

*Strive for full restoration, encourage one another,
be of one mind, live in peace. And the God
of love and peace will be with you.*

2 Corinthians 13:11 niv

No one enjoys division, least of all Me. I created My children to live in unity and harmony. It breaks My heart when friends part ways, especially when unnecessary pride is involved. I know it hurts your heart, too. I've seen the impact that friendship rifts have had on you. They've left you confused and grieving. What did you do to deserve the pain you received, and from someone you trusted no less? How can you keep it from ever happening again? You're even questioning your ability to be a good friend to others. *Is there something wrong with me? Why don't people want to maintain healthy relationships with me? Will all my friendships end this way?* Here's the truth: you are lovable and worthy of befriending. I long to be the kind of friend who teaches you the meaning of the words *sticking power*. Instead of focusing on those who didn't hang around, look to Me. I'll be here, even on your bad days. I can stick with you, even when you're ready to bolt. You won't want to bolt, though. We'll have so many great times together that leaving Me will be the last thing on your mind. So grab My hand. Let's do this friendship thing together.

Marital Separation

My flesh and my heart may fail, but God is the strength of my heart and my portion forever.

PSALM 73:26 NIV

The pain of separation is a deep one. I know, because there have been so many times when My children have pulled away from Me. I'm not keen on division, but there are times in every relationship when it's good to pull away for a season of prayer and reflection. I had to do this in the garden on the night I was betrayed. I pulled away from My disciples so that I could have some alone time with My Father. This wasn't a selfish move on My part. In fact, it was critical. Your alone time could turn out to be critical as well. Just remember to use this period to draw near to Me, to seek My face, and to get My input on your situation. Don't try to force the hand of your spouse. In fact, just leave him in My care. I promise, I can do the necessary work. Remember, I long for the two of you to be one. But each one has to be whole, not half. So let Me work on smoothing out the rough edges in both of you before I piece things back together. You'll be glad you took the time to allow Me to do this important work.

LOSS OF PURITY

Now for this very reason also, applying all diligence, in your faith supply moral excellence, and in your moral excellence, knowledge, and in your knowledge, self-control, and in your self-control, perseverance, and in your perseverance, godliness, and in your godliness, brotherly kindness, and in your brotherly kindness, love.

2 PETER 1:5–7 NASB

You've reached a crossroads in a relationship. Things have taken a turn in a direction you never planned to go. You crossed one line and then another. Now you find yourself grieving the loss of your purity, your virtue. You're ashamed that things have moved in this direction, and you don't know how to turn back the clock. Can your sins be washed cleaned? How do you keep from giving in to that temptation again? Can you really get this train back on track? Will you have to end the relationship to do so? Sweet girl, I long to wash you white as snow, to take things back to the way they were before you headed down this slippery slope. Confess your sins, and I will be just to forgive them. That's My promise. You can see virtue restored. You can see shame washed away along with every sin. With My help you really can turn this situation around without causing any more pain.

LONG LIFE

. . . .

*"With long life I will satisfy him
and show him my salvation."*

PSALM 91:16 NIV

You've lost a grandparent. Though you know this was an inevitable transition, your heart is broken. What a blessing to love and care for this special family member, to hear her stories about days gone by. To see that wrinkled skin, those gnarled fingers, that wispy white hair. She was a hidden treasure, a wealth of knowledge. And now her sudden passing has taken you by surprise. I understand those feelings. The loss of someone you love is difficult, especially someone as loving and kind as this. I want you to know that she's safe with Me now and having a grand time. Talk about a perfect fit for heaven! She's no longer carrying the burden of age. Instead, she is young and blissfully carefree. She's also pain free, and her memory is fully intact. Oh, how I wish you could see her. If you could, you'd stop grieving in an instant! Soon enough, it will all be made clear to you. In the meantime, I'd like to encourage you to celebrate the long and precious life she lived. What a blessing she was to so many!

STATUTE OF LIMITATIONS

* *

*How long, O LORD? Will you forget me
forever? How long will you hide
your face from me?*

PSALM 13:1 ESV

Grief has no statute of limitations. I know people are trying to convince you otherwise, but they aren't living your story. They're not facing the same loss you've faced. Their suggestions to "get over it" are well intended, but they don't really know what you're thinking and feeling. I do. I know. I care. In fact, the kind of caring I offer is the sort that allows you to get to the core of the pain, to face it for what it is. I'll be here with you, no matter how long it takes to make it through the various stages of the grieving process. No condemnation. No wagging fingers. I'll be the One who helps you heal. I know a little something about healing, you see. I've been in the healing business from the very beginning of time. So don't stress over the calendar. Don't give your grief an end date. Sure, I want to see you healed, but I also need you to understand that what you're thinking and feeling is completely natural and normal after facing such a tough loss. My heart is with you. You will get through this, no matter how long it takes.

Health Issues

. . . .

If your law had not been my delight,
I would have perished in my affliction.

Psalm 119:92 niv

I see your concerns. I hear those *What's coming next?* thoughts running through your mind. You've been concerned about your health for some time now. You've noticed symptoms. Things aren't as they should be, and you're already grieving, wondering if the days of good health are behind you. A trip to the doctor has added even more fears as he runs tests to figure out what's going on. He seems concerned. In the still of the night, fear grips you. You scour the Internet, reading articles and trying to figure things out. You imagine the worst. Will this illness take you down? Oh, My sweet child, how I care about what you're going through. Remember, you are created in My image. I care very much about your physical body. Reach out to Me. Trust Me. Let Me show you how to navigate this season. And don't stop praying for healing. It's My good pleasure to give good gifts to My children. Healing is one of those gifts. So lift your eyes and your heart. Begin to praise Me and watch how I perform on your behalf.

Abandonment from a Romantic Relationship

. . . .

"Be strong and courageous. Do not be afraid or terrified because of them, for the LORD your God goes with you; he will never leave you nor forsake you."

DEUTERONOMY 31:6 NIV

Oh, the wonderful dreams you had about romance. You pictured your story much like a romance novel, with the hero sweeping you off your feet and carrying you into the sunset for a storybook happily-ever-after. Now you feel as though you've been swept off your feet in a whole different way. "Knocked senseless" might be more like it. Just about the time you were convinced he was Prince Charming, he decided to skip out on the relationship. No explanation. No particular reason. He just decided it wasn't for him. You're broken. You're confused. The image you had in your head isn't matching up with your current reality. Now what? Daughter, I stand before you, robed in white, ready to take your hand. You are My bride. I am the one true Prince. If you'll begin to see Me as who I really am, you'll find a relationship that far surpasses the one you've just lost. I will never get bored. I will never turn My eye to another. I'll sweep you off your feet and carry you off into the very best sort of happily-ever-after you could imagine.

PSYCHOLOGICAL IMPRISONMENT
OF A LOVED ONE

. . . .

*For the LORD hears the needy and does
not despise his own people who are prisoners.*

PSALM 69:33 ESV

When your loved one faces a mental challenge or psychological imprisonment, it can be devastating to watch. The inner turmoil can manifest in frightening external ways. It can be tough to participate in the ups and downs. Your life can shift from normal to topsy-turvy from second to second, depending on how that person is handling the current crisis. Emotional upheavals rule the day, and the journey can become perplexing, even terrifying. You grieve the loved one who once seemed so. . .normal. She's anything but, now. In fact, her erratic behavior frightens you. You're not sure how to fix this. Should you try? Recommend professional help? Or should you back away from the fire to save yourself and those you love? Sweet girl, I care about your loved one so much. I want to see her mind healed as well as her heart. Don't give up. Don't stop praying for her. I'm moving on her behalf and would love it if you would stick with Me as I bring My plans to fulfillment in her life. We can see her set free from this bondage. It's My ultimate goal, so don't give up.

CHANGE IN HEALTH

*My comfort in my suffering is this:
your promise preserves my life.*

PSALM 119:50 NIV

The human body was made to bear up under a lot of pressure. You've taken that for granted by overdoing it. Lately, things are out of control. You've worn yourself to a thread. Going, going, going has caused your health to wane. Your body is beginning to change. Little aches and pains are more exaggerated. Things that weren't problematic a few months ago are now really bothering you. You're struggling to put into words the way you feel, but it's not good. Even the doctor seems to be perplexed at your symptoms. Others have turned a blind eye, as if they think you're exaggerating, but you know better. You just want things to go back to how they were. I care so much about your body. I created it, after all. And I want to see every joint, every muscle, every organ in perfect alignment. So look to Me, the Author of your faith, as you seek healing. Get the medical care you need, of course, but don't leave Me out of the equation. Ask. Seek. Knock. I'm right here, waiting to answer.

THE ONES WHO REMAIN

Bear one another's burdens,
and thereby fulfill the law of Christ.

GALATIANS 6:2 NASB

You're feeling hollow. Empty. You can't stop thinking about the one you've lost. I understand the pain, but I want to remind you of the ones who remain. They need you. They love you. They miss you. They're grieving the loss of *you*, since you've slipped into such a deep state of grief. They miss the old days when you were able to enjoy life, to laugh, to play. They wish you had more time to focus on yourself and on them. In short, they want you back. They want to see you restored in every conceivable way. I want the very same thing for you Myself. I want to bring you back among the living so that you can continue in relationship with those who remain. Will you let Me do that? There are better days ahead. And though it's hard to imagine, there will be fun days ahead with those you love. They're waiting for this, even now. Shift your gaze to them when you are able. You'll find that they're standing nearby, hands extended, to enter the next phase of life with you.

LOSING SLEEP

In peace I will lie down and sleep,
for you alone, LORD, make me dwell in safety.

PSALM 4:8 NIV

I see you tossing and turning in your bed. Troubling thoughts keep you awake. In the still of the night, when others are comfortably dozing, you're wrestling with the covers and trying to figure out how to make unworkable situations work. Instead of resting your heart, body, and mind, you're riddled with anxiety. You're trying to come up with a plan. Then morning comes and you drag yourself out of bed, exhausted and battle weary. Midday, you find yourself grieving the loss of peace and rest. Oh, how I wish you could calm your heart so that you could sleep. I designed your body to need rest, and you're not getting enough. That's certainly not helping your situation any. Can you trust Me, child? Can you truly believe—even in the middle of the night—that I'm going to fix those things that need fixing? I will, you know. What you cannot do (in the natural), I'm happy to do in the supernatural. Stand back and watch Me move on your behalf, then be prepared to get the rest you need as you leave matters in My hands.

MINISTRY OF CARING

For he says to Moses, "I will have mercy
on whom I have mercy, and I will have
compassion on whom I have compassion."

ROMANS 9:15 NIV

You're in the compassion business, whether you meant to be or not. All ministry workers are. You see hurting people on a daily basis. They come into the church to pour out their hearts. You dry their tears. You pray for them. You offer hugs, condolences, love, affection. But there's only so much you can do. You leave those situations feeling drained and wondering if your words helped. . .at all. Let Me assure you, child, they did. Comfort is never wasted. Compassion is never in vain. When people are hurting, they need someone to wrap them into a warm hug and say, "You're going to make it." You've been that person to many, and they sense your genuine love. And though you would never consider yourself as such, you've been a minister all along. You are, after all, ministering to the needs of others, putting their hurts above your own. It takes a special kind of woman to give so freely of herself, and I want you to know that I see and I'm proud of you.

PERCEIVED LOSSES

* *

Submit yourselves, then, to God.
Resist the devil, and he will flee from you.

JAMES 4:7 NIV

What a materialistic place the world has become. I did
not create it to be this way, but look around you and
you'll see that everyone is striving for stuff. They want
bigger. They want better. They want more. Magazines and
television commercials advertise the ultimate lifestyle,
one loaded with possessions, possessions, and more
possessions. Fancy cars. Luxury vacation homes. Nice
clothes. Expensive grooming products. You see photos
of people who've become financially successful, and you
secretly wish you could have what they have (or at least
what they *seem* to have). Oh, you don't say it out-loud, but
the thoughts cross your mind: *Why can't I go on vacations?*
Why doesn't my house look like that? Why aren't my clothes
nice like hers? You grieve your perceived "losses" (the things
you think you'll never have) and wonder why you've been
cheated. You haven't been cheated at all, child. In fact, you
have more than most, because you have the promise of
eternity. You couldn't trade that for all the riches in the
world! So be satisfied. Don't envy. Then watch as I change
your perspective to show you that you have already gained
all you will ever need and more.

WATCHING SOMEONE FADE
BEFORE YOUR EYES

. . . .

Do not cast me off in the time of old age;
forsake me not when my strength is spent.

PSALM 71:9 ESV

She's fading before your eyes. Yesterday she knew your name. In fact, she knew everything about you. She raised you, after all—changed your diapers, packed your school lunches, wiped your tears, and sewed your clothes. Now she stares at you with a blank expression, completely lost. You're perplexed by this behavior. Scared, even. Just months ago she could dress herself. Now she struggles to put on a shirt without help. Watching your loved one slip into the abyss of dementia or Alzheimer's can be terrifying. As her memories (and abilities) fade, your hope tends to follow suit. Oh, My daughter, I am so proud of you for sticking close to the one in need. You're showing her My heart every time you wash her face, help give medications, or guide her from room to room. It's My love you're sharing. So don't give up. Don't give in to fear. Even in the midst of this very difficult journey I will show Myself strong. And I'll teach you to be strong, too. I know you don't feel very strong right now. But I'm growing you from the inside out. Don't grieve this difficult season. Square those shoulders. Do what needs to be done. We'll get through this together.

WEIGHT GAIN

. . . .

I have been crucified with Christ. It is no longer I who live, but Christ who lives in me. And the life I now live in the flesh I live by faith in the Son of God, who loved me and gave himself for me.

You've lost the weight before. It felt really good, too. You enjoyed the admiring looks, the encouraging comments, and the feeling you had when you looked in the mirror. Now you want to toss the mirror into the nearest Dumpster. Things have unraveled in a major way. You're ashamed, you're embarrassed, and you're grieving the thinner version of you. Photos from last year—or the year before—send you into the pits of despair. How did you get from that version of yourself to the one staring you in the mirror right now? Can you turn back the hands of time? I know you're disappointed, but remember that I love you regardless of your weight. It's true. Sure, I want you to be healthy, but don't spend so much time focusing on what you wish you looked like. Instead, pay more attention to the inner you. I'd love to see that inner girl beefed up. Give her some spiritual muscle. Don't let her waste away. When you've got that girl in shape, we can start to talk about the outside. Maybe. Or maybe we'll just hang out together so I can teach you to love the woman you are, cellulite and all.

A Man of Sorrows

. . . .

He was despised and rejected by mankind,
a man of suffering, and familiar with pain.
Like one from whom people hide their faces he
was despised, and we held him in low esteem.

ISAIAH 53:3 NIV

I see the sorrow you've faced. It's been deep, agonizing. You've never felt so low, so lost. I want you to know, My child, that I understand. Even before I came to this earth, prophets were already speaking deep words about Me. They called Me "a man of sorrows, and acquainted with grief" (KJV). They weren't describing My countenance. It's not that I was downcast all the time. Far from it. But I faced the deepest kind of sorrows: rejection from those I loved, suffering on the cross, and death at the hands of people who despised Me. They held Me in low esteem. They considered Me worthless. So trust Me when I say that I understand what you're feeling as you walk through the valley. But remember, My story ended on a very high note. On the third day I rose from the grave. My resurrection was a triumphant "Amen!" that put an end to the suffering. Once and for all, it proved that I was who I said I was and that I could do what I said I could do. You're capable of great things, too, so don't linger in your grave clothes for long. It's time to rise up and face your destiny on this side of the sorrow.

PARENTAL ABANDONMENT

*For the LORD your God is a merciful God;
he will not abandon or destroy you or forget
the covenant with your ancestors,
which he confirmed to them by oath.*

DEUTERONOMY 4:31 NIV

It makes no sense to you at all. Parents are supposed to stay. They're not supposed to leave you or shift their attention to a new family. How can the people who once nurtured you turn their back on you, pretend you don't even exist? Was it something you did? Were you not good enough? And how can they shift all of their focus to a brand-new family, giving them the things you never had? It's so unfair. They're doing fun and exciting things that they never did with you. You're confused, but you're also hurting. Are you being petty? Selfish? They seem so happy now, as if they don't even realize how hurtful all of this is to you. It doesn't seem like a good time to confront them, not when they seem so deliriously happy with their new family. But there are so many things you want to say! Oh, sweet girl. . .say them to Me. Tell Me all about how you're grieving. Cry out with the pain of what you're experiencing and the feelings of betrayal you're battling. I can take it. And while we're spending time together, I'll show you what a real parent looks like. I won't shift My gaze from you. I won't prefer one above another. I'll just go on loving you as the precious child you are—and always will be.

More Than You Can Imagine

*Now to Him who is able to do far more
abundantly beyond all that we ask or think,
according to the power that works within us,
to Him be the glory in the church and in Christ
Jesus to all generations forever and ever. Amen.*

Ephesians 3:20–21 nasb

You're tired of operating in your own strength. You're worn out. What's the point of working so hard, giving 110 percent, when you don't see the payoff you hoped for? You just end up tired and frustrated, and no one seems to understand. I get it. You're grieving the days when you felt energetic and strong. You wish you could figure out a plan that would work for the long term instead of just sticking bandages on everything to stop the bleeding. Operating this way has worn you to a thread. These days, you're doing well just to crawl out of bed and drag from place to place. If only you could regroup. Think. Plan. But that would take energy you just don't have right now. Remember, child: When you are at your weakest, I'm able to move on your behalf. I don't just move; I go above and beyond. That's what happens when you let go and trust Me. I'm able to do exceedingly abundantly above all that you could ask (so ask away) or think (keep those positive thoughts coming). I love you, dear one. I want to see you rested and energetic, capable of making wise decisions. And it makes Me happy to do more than you could ever imagine.

Your Tribe

*No one has ever seen God; but if we love
one another, God lives in us and his
love is made complete in us.*

1 John 4:12 niv

I designed you to live in community. Relationships are key to your success. All My children need to be surrounded by people who will give support, love, and encouragement. I called twelve people into My inner circle, men I trusted to walk with Me, no matter how difficult the journey. Without My tribe, My disciples, My journey would have been much more difficult. The same is true for you. If you're trying to do life on your own, without the support of your spiritual mentors and peers, then you're missing out. You'll end up leaning too much on self and not the comfort and advice of others. So who are the folks in your tribe? Easy. . .those who naturally gravitate to you, giving pats on the back. If you're going through a particularly rough season (or grieving a loss), pull together your team and ask them to pray. If you need direction, ask for godly input. And if you're feeling lonely, begin to seek out the shoulder of a tribe member who cares. They love you, you know. I've poured a special love in each heart, just for you.

A Caregiver's Loss of Freedom

"*In all things I have shown you that by working hard in this way we must help the weak and remember the words of the Lord Jesus, how he himself said, 'It is more blessed to give than to receive.'*"

ACTS 20:35 ESV

The loss of freedom can be particularly tough when you feel trapped in a situation that is beyond your control. Oh, how you long for the old days, when you could pick up a phone and call a friend then meet her for dinner and a movie. You're wishing you could take a drive to clear your mind, but you can't leave the person you're caring for. My child, it's time for a break. You need help. Instead of taking this entire load upon your shoulders, let Me show you whom to reach out to. There are people in the wings, ready for this very moment, to guide you, assist you, and offer encouragement and comfort. Begin to take back your freedom, just a few moments at a time. Watch the feelings of imprisonment fade away. Enjoy the possibilities again. Go to lunch with that friend, even if it means you have to hire someone to watch your loved one. Call a buddy on the phone and cry if you need to. Cast off the bondage this situation has created in your mind, and look for ways to live in balance. I'll help you every step of the way.

Death of a Friend

. . . .

Listen, I tell you a mystery: We will not all sleep, but we will all be changed.

1 Corinthians 15:51 niv

A beloved friend has passed away. This loss has devastated you. She was your first phone call, the one you shared all your secrets and deepest longings with. She was the one who patted you on the back when you succeeded, and gave you what for when you bumbled. And now she's not here. You pick up the phone, wishing you could make a call, but she won't answer. Your home is filled with things that she gave you: silly cards, little trinkets, birthday presents—funny, quirky things that make you think of her every time you turn around. The things remain, but she does not. You need a shoulder to cry on, but hers is no longer available. There will come a day when you will see her again. She is healed and whole now. And all those hours you spent swapping stories and leaning on each other? Those days aren't over. When you're reunited, you'll have a lot of catching up to do, but the love will remain. So don't grieve for long. Turn your eyes toward heaven and begin to live for eternity, when we'll be one big happy family.

DAILY ENCOURAGEMENT

Your love has given me great joy
and encouragement, because you, brother,
have refreshed the hearts of the Lord's people.

PHILEMON 1:7 NIV

Oh, how you long for encouragers in your life. You would love to have faith-speaking, uplifting folks pop in for an encouraging word or two. Instead, you're surrounded by naysayers—people who see the glass as half-empty. They're more than happy to speak into your life, but their words are as weighty as a blanket. You wonder if the helpful, happy people are all busy speaking into other people's lives. Here's a great piece of advice, child. Become that person you wish others would be for you. Skip the negativity. Speak words of life and love over your friends. Be the encourager in the group. Don't let the bad seed of negativity take root. People will see that you are a glass-half-full kind of gal and will respond in kind. Their negativity will be a glaring contrast to the kind of words streaming from your mouth. And guess what? Those positive words coming from your mouth? They might just be all the encouragement you need to get through the battles you face. In other words, you can be your own encouraging friend!

A New Season Coming

. . . .

There is a time for everything, and a season
for every activity under the heavens.

ECCLESIASTES 3:1 NIV

You're wondering about the seasons of your life. Specifically, you're hoping the one you're now walking through won't drag on and on. It's been a particularly difficult season, and you're ready to be done with it. In fact, you wish you'd never walked through it at all. You wonder if the grieving will ever come to an end. Remember, My child, that springtime wouldn't feel like springtime if it didn't come on the heels of winter. If the ground underneath your feet wasn't frozen, you wouldn't appreciate the thawing. Yes, winter can be a challenge, but it's not a forever season. That's the problem with seasons: you always seem to forget they're temporary. I can absolutely assure you of this: Springtime is coming sooner than you think. It's fresh on the heels of what you're trudging through. Even now, little buds are popping up on the trees, and hope is in the air. Things won't stay frozen and hard for long. Begin to look at this next season with expectation. Have a sense of excitement about what's coming around the bend. Anticipate the best from Me. . .and you will surely see it come to pass.

Your Child Getting Married

. . . .

Train up a child in the way he should go,
even when he is old he will not depart from it.

PROVERBS 22:6 NASB

It's impossible to imagine, but your child is getting married. You're excited for him, of course, but you're also grieving. He'll be moving away for good this time. His attentions will be on his new wife, as they should be. Will he forget you? Will Christmas plans have to change? And what about birthdays? How will any celebration be the same if you're not coordinating it? Will your house feel like home, now that his bedroom has been converted into a guest room? This is a complex season, isn't it? Your job as a mom was to get that son to adulthood and to make sure he turned out to be a responsible man who loved Me, his Savior. You did a fantastic job, Mom. And you did a fine job of training him up to love and care for his new wife. Give yourself a pat on the back for growing him into a mighty man of God. Your work isn't over, but your job description is changing. Embrace these changes. And don't stop praying for him. He's got a big job ahead: husband, future daddy, and provider for that new family of his. He's going to need a praying mama, like he always did.

GRIEF OVER SIN

For we know that our old self was crucified
with him so that the body ruled by sin might
be done away with, that we should
no longer be slaves to sin.

ROMANS 6:6 NIV

You didn't mean to get caught up in sin, but here you are, feeling trapped. It has wound its tentacles around you, and you can't seem to breathe. Your actions are contrary to what you believe—even what you want to do—but you can't seem to help yourself. You're driven back to the same thing that has held you bound in the past, and you're grieving it every step of the way. You try to escape using your own strength but cannot seem to bend the bars of the cell that holds you bound. Oh, My child, how I long for you to be set free. There's no need to grieve. I can deliver you, once and for all. It's not a matter of trying hard enough; it's a matter of trusting Me enough. I can do, in one instant, what you have been unable to do on your own. I never meant for you to fight this battle alone. I'm right here, ready to move on your behalf. Are you ready? If so, take My hand, and let's take the very first step toward freedom. . .together.

MENDED

A time to tear and a time to mend,
a time to be silent and a time to speak.

ECCLESIASTES 3:7 NIV

There have been many shattered places in your life over the years. In some ways you feel like a broken vase that has been glued back together. Tiny shards of glass remain on the floor, causing a hazard as you move about. Every now and again, pain seeps through the cracks in the vase. Other times you're like a torn blouse that's been mended. The stitches are obvious to the outside world. Oh, but don't you see, daughter? Those stitches are part of the design. They're what make you. . .you. You're uniquely crafted and uniquely mended. I've done a spectacular (and creative) job of putting things back together for you. So don't grieve the fact that there are exposed places. You wouldn't be human if every little stitch was perfect. You wouldn't have to depend on Me if the vase didn't leak. I'm in the business of putting things back together, so trust Me during this process, even if it seems a little painful at times. And don't worry too much about what others think about your situation. They have their own cracks, their own stitches. Whether you realize it or not, all My kids are cracked pots, held together by My Spirit.

I'm Always Speaking

For the word of God is living and active,
sharper than any two-edged sword, piercing to the
division of soul and of spirit, of joints and
of marrow, and discerning the thought
and intentions of the heart.

HEBREWS 4:12 ESV

You wonder if I'm speaking to you. You've cried out to Me, expressed your grief, your pain, and yet you're convinced I've remained silent. This angers you. It makes no sense. Why won't I say something to make sense of this mess you're in? Have I abandoned you? Oh, dear one, I'm still speaking—whether you hear the words or not. Open the pages of that dusty Bible. Look for My thoughts, My words on your situation. You'll find everything you're looking for there. Yes, I still speak directly to the hearts of My children, but you'll find that My Word has every answer you could ever need. Its pages are filled with stories of people, just like you, who overcame the very same obstacles you're facing now. Read about their lives. Study their journeys. Gain insight into your situation. I will speak through those stories and give you nuggets of wisdom that you can use to transition from one stage to another. I'm speaking, even now, wooing you to open that Bible. *Shh.* Listen. Can you hear Me?

THE LORD WILL PROVIDE

. . . .

For the LORD God is a sun and shield;
the LORD bestows favor and honor.
No good thing does he withhold
from those who walk uprightly.

PSALM 84:11 ESV

You're grieving the loss of income. Not so long ago you had everything you needed. Today? It's disappeared like a puff of smoke. I see how much it hurts not to be able to take care of things like you once did. You long for the days of paying bills on time. You wish you didn't have to fend off calls from bill collectors. Most of all, you long for the days of peace and rest. Right now you're working so hard with little payoff. This is one of those times, My child, when I want to encourage you to trust Me in the seasons. I am your provider. Read those words again: I am your provider. I know that concept makes little sense. I'm not the one who is working the job, making the deposits, and writing the checks. I'm not the one getting up at the crack of dawn, juggling home, family, and work. But I'm the One arranging it all behind the scenes. You can trust Me. I am a good Father, and I want to make sure My children have everything they need in order to live successful lives. So trust Me as you once trusted your dad to provide for you. I'm not in the business of withholding. I'm in the business of caring.

ECHOES OF LONELINESS

*"Sing, barren woman, you who never bore
a child; burst into song, shout for joy,
you who were never in labor; because more are
the children of the desolate woman than of
her who has a husband," says the LORD.*

ISAIAH 54:1 NIV

It's an ache that never seems to lessen: an empty womb. And it's not the only thing feeling empty these days. Your heart is a big, vacant oil drum with endless echoes of loneliness. Though you would never speak the word aloud, you feel like a failure. Why won't your body cooperate? Why are you lacking? Why are your friends bearing children—some, one after the other—when you can't? I hear these questions. I also hear your cries in the night: *God, why don't You do something? I want a child so desperately. I would do anything to cradle a baby in my arms, but You won't give me one. You can fill the empty spaces, Lord, but You don't want to. What have I done to deserve this?* I want you to know that I do fill the empty spaces, but I start with the heart. And, child, you've done nothing to deserve the evil that this world dishes out. This isn't some sort of personal vendetta on My part. I long to fill every void. I also long to take the barren, broken heart and make it whole again. So start there. Give Me that fractured heart. Let Me mend it, and we'll begin to work on the deep, unspoken longings after that.

YOUR CHILD'S PATH

You make known to me the path of life;
you will fill me with joy in your presence,
with eternal pleasures at your right hand.

PSALM 16:11 NIV

I see that broken heart, Mama. Your child is different. He can't do what other children can do. He can't learn like other children can learn. He struggles to fit in, and you're already fretting over what his life will be like in adulthood. Many times you've wept as you've watched him struggle. It doesn't seem fair. You hate to use the word *disabled*, but there are moments when you whisper it under your breath. Why this child? Why this juncture in your life? How can you possibly give him all that he needs to be fully successful? Where do you start? Oh, Mama! He's specially-abled! Watch and see how I use this very unique child of yours. He's going to go places. He's going to show people things. He'll teach life lessons. And he'll have a rich, full life in Me. There's no lack when it comes to his spirit. I'm in constant communication with that child of yours, whispering to his heart, giving attaboys when he's facing the tough stuff. So hang on for the ride and watch how high he climbs. He might just surprise you.

ABUNDANT LIFE

"The thief comes only to steal and kill and destroy. I came that they may have life and have it abundantly."

JOHN 10:10 ESV

I hear the quiet cries of your heart. You want more from life. You feel cheated and secretly wonder why others have it better than you do. You read My Word. You see the scriptures that say I want you to have abundant life, but you don't feel like *abundance* is a word you can relate to. Instead, you feel taken advantage of. Your life is hard. Others don't have to work as hard as you do, and they have lovely homes, nice cars, and plenty of food on the table. They're living the "abundant" life. Why is everything so much tougher for you? Oh, My sweet child. . .I will make sure you have all you need. Begin to praise Me, even now. Give Me your deepest desires. Don't crave material things, but don't doubt My ability to fulfill your longings, either. And keep your focus on Me. Don't spend too much time staring at what your neighbor has. I'm working out a few issues with her, too. I'm working on all of you to bring the kind of abundance that really matters: a full and rich life in Me.

Spending More Time
with Your Kids

*So the ransomed of the LORD will return
and come with joyful shouting to Zion,
and everlasting joy will be on their heads.*

Isaiah 51:11 NASB

It's happening again, isn't it, My child? You're noticing that some of your friends have more time with their children than you do. They don't have to work full-time jobs. They don't sit in evening traffic. They're not always rushing, rushing, rushing just to make ends meet. They prepare home-cooked meals, hot from the oven, while you pick up fast-food chicken nuggets or burgers. . .again. And while you appreciate your job, you secretly wish you had more time to just be Mom. Let Me start by telling you that you're a great mom. Everything you do, you do for the ones you love. I see that, and they do, too. So never doubt that. I also need to tell you that I see the desires of your heart and am working on many plans for you to enjoy fun times with your family. Take advantage of the little moments. Enjoy weekend road trips. Make plans for bigger vacations. Begin to think about the things you'd like to do and then ask Me to show you how we can accomplish them together. You're the epitome of one who cares enough to work hard for those you adore, and I love that about you.

Aimless Wandering

*I have gone astray like a lost sheep;
seek Your servant, for I do not
forget Your commandments.*

PSALM 119:176 NASB

You're feeling lost, like a wanderer without a home. Nothing inside of you feels settled. You're not completely at home anywhere—at your job, your church, even your house. And though you can't put your finger on it, you don't feel at home with some of the people in your life, either. When you analyze why you feel this way, you can't seem to come up with a logical explanation. You're grieving the lack of stability. I know the answer, child. You're not rooted in your relationship with Me. When you're truly at home with Me, your Father, I'll help you settle into your job, your house, your relationships. How do you become rooted? Begin to spend more time with Me. Look at your schedule—really look at it—and write down a time of day that makes sense for carving out time with Me. Then draw close during that special time of day. Pour out your heart. Ask My opinion. Listen for My responses. Feel My heart beating over your situation. I promise, I'll begin to settle your spirit. Those restless feelings? I'll take charge of them and will settle you down. So draw near. Let's put those wandering days behind you, once and for all.

Richly Loved

But because of his great love for us, God,
who is rich in mercy, made us alive with Christ
even when we were dead in transgressions—
it is by grace you have been saved.

Ephesians 2:4–5 NIV

There are days when you don't feel loved. Your heart aches because you wonder if anyone cares. You grieve the loss of compassionate responses to the challenges you face. To your way of thinking, you are much kinder to others than they are to you. You look around at how busy and distracted your loved ones are and realize they simply don't have time or energy to deal with your problems. Oh, but I do, precious child. I have plenty of time. And even though your friends and family members are negligent in showing love, I'll never be! You are richly loved by your heavenly Father. You are alive in Me. Even when you were dead in your sins and transgressions, My grace saved you. So don't look to others to fill the gap in your heart. Don't get angry when their responses aren't what you'd hoped or expected. Simply look to Me. I'm right here, arms open wide, ready to convince you of My everlasting love, which will stand the test of time and will guide you through every rough patch.

BUSYNESS

. . . .

Look carefully then how you walk, not as unwise
but as wise, making the best use of the time,
because the days are evil. Therefore do not
be foolish, but understand what
the will of the Lord is.

EPHESIANS 5:15–17 ESV

You want to slow down. Your schedule is whirling out of control. Your to-do list is so long you have to invest in more paper. I see how crazy things are for you right now, daughter. I also see that you're quietly grieving the old days when life moved at a slower pace. Not that you have time to really fret over it for long, of course. You're always plowing forward, getting that next task done—driving the kids to gymnastics, pushing through morning traffic to get to a meeting, buzzing through the fast-food restaurant to shovel down a quick lunch. Today I'd love it if you would hit the PAUSE button for a few precious minutes with Me. I can talk to you, no matter where you are—in the car, in the shower, in the drive-through lane. But I do want to have a little chat. I'd like to share some ideas about how we can slow things down a bit, possibly even let go of a few activities. I'd like to remind you that spending time with Me will prepare you for all those other tasks you want to accomplish. I'm whispering some thoughts about that very thing right now, in this very moment. Are you listening? Won't you take the time?

SIGHTLESS

. . . .

For we live by faith, not by sight.

2 CORINTHIANS 5:7 NIV

You're doing your best not to live by sight. Unfortunately, there are so many things staring you in the face that you're finding it difficult. Every time you turn around you see bills piling up, a late mortgage payment, squabbling children, marriage woes, strained friendships, and more. These things are hard to ignore, though you squeeze your eyes shut to a few of them on occasion. You can't depend on your feelings, either. You're riddled with confusion and doubt despite your best attempts to keep the faith. You keep looking for a burst of sunlight to break through over the horizon, but it's late in coming (or too far away to see). Oh, dear one, don't look with your earthly eyes. If you really want to find hope for the future (and for your current situation), try to take a peek at your situation through My eyes. I see all. I see the good news coming around the bend. I see how much your heart has grown. I see people sweeping in around you to pray and to lift your arms. I see angels taking their stance in every corner of your home. So ask for My vision today. I'll give you a peek if you're really interested in seeing something that will knock your socks off. I'm peeling back the veil, even now.

FORGIVEN, SET FREE

If we confess our sins, he is faithful
and just to forgive us our sins and to
cleanse us from all unrighteousness.

1 JOHN 1:9 ESV

I see the relief written all over your face. You're so glad to have shaken off the past with all of its drama, pain, and mistakes. For the first time you understand the word *freedom*. It's a word that sends your heart in a completely different direction from before. You're relishing this new season, where you fully recognize and appreciate the forgiveness I offered on the cross. What a huge relief to finally let go and let Me take the reins. This makes My heart so happy. I love to see My kids set free—from poor choices, addictions, bad relationships, and sin in general. Just one word of advice: be on the lookout for the enemy, even now. He likes to prowl around, wreaking havoc. He strikes when you least expect it. He'll attempt to bring condemnation and inner turmoil if you let him. Don't let him. Turn your eyes toward heaven. Remember what My freedom, My forgiveness, feels like. You'll have nothing to grieve if you keep your focus on My promises. That's what freedom is all about!

INABILITY TO CONCEIVE

In her deep anguish Hannah prayed to the
LORD, weeping bitterly. And she made a vow,
saying, "LORD Almighty, if you will only look
on your servant's misery and remember me,
and not forget your servant but give her a son,
then I will give him to the LORD for
all the days of his life."

1 SAMUEL 1:10–11 NIV

I see your heart, daughter. You long for a child. You grieve for a child. You envision the child that is to come. You've designed the room. You've got your grandmother's cradle. But there's no baby to put inside of it. You can't help but stop and look at layette items. But there's no little one to dress. And you wonder if there ever will be. Please know how much I love you and how I long to fulfill your desires. Sometimes I wish you could see what's coming around the bend like I can, because then you would know that I've got amazing things in store for you. I am an arm-filling God. I'll say that again so that you really believe it. I am an arm-filling—and heart-filling—God. It was never My intention to leave you empty armed or empty hearted. I'm not here to rob you of joy and fulfillment. I have such fun ways to fill those arms, so trust Me throughout this journey. I am trustworthy, you know. That will never, ever change. Neither will My deep, abiding love for you, My daughter.

DON'T SUPPRESS

I love the LORD, for he heard my voice;
he heard my cry for mercy. Because he turned
his ear to me, I will call on him
as long as I live.

PSALM 116:1–2 NIV

Whew! That's hard work, girl! You're spending a lot of time avoiding the grief, aren't you? You do your best to tuck it away so that you don't feel anything. It's better to just be numb. That's your motto, anyway. But I'm here to tell you that suppressing never ends well. In order to be fully healed, you've got to acknowledge the grief. Allow yourself to walk through the various stages. So let it out. Let the aches, the pain, the heartache have their say. With My help, those wounds will heal. If you continue to suppress, suppress, suppress, you'll end up sick, physically and psychologically. I've given you grief as a gift. (I know, I know. . .it doesn't feel like much of a gift, does it?) But it's true. Without grief, the human body couldn't contain the agony of loss. Let it out through tears. Let it out through anger. Let it out in whatever way it comes. These moments of release will help you in the long run, I promise. Instead of imploding, you will eventually feel the peace that comes with release. So let's get started. Okay? Deep breath now. We're in this together.

My Inheritance

For the LORD will not abandon His people,
nor will He forsake His inheritance.

PSALM 94:14 NASB

❦

You are My inheritance. You're My legacy. And because you're My offspring (My people, as it were) I won't ever abandon you. You're the gift I've left behind to the world, the ones who will carry on the plans I started. Maybe you don't always feel like you've got the goods. You don't feel like much of a legacy. You grieve the fact that you're not "as gifted as" or "as pretty as" some of My other kids. In the quiet times you wonder if you're doing My name justice because you never seem to say the right things at the right times or perform up to par (according to your standards, not Mine). Oh, but you are! Please don't compare yourself to others. I've made you all different for a reason. The people you'll reach? No one else could reach them but you. Trust Me when I say that I'm up to something here, and you're definitely a part of it, flaws and all. I'm tickled pink that you're My inheritance. You're the "Me" the world is watching. . .Jesus with skin on. And I did a great job of handpicking you for the job. What a treasure you are, daughter! What a legacy!

STYLES OF WORSHIP

And above all these put on love,
which binds everything together in
perfect harmony.

COLOSSIANS 3:14 ESV

You're in a new church. Their style of worship is different. Unusual. It's not what you're used to. In the old church, you'd grown accustomed to the type of music, the voices, the harmonies. The sound levels were different. The instruments were different. Even the sermon style is different in your new church home. The pastor's tone, inflections, and style aren't what you're used to. Even his sense of humor (or lack thereof) is off-putting. There are times when these things really bother you. You preferred the old ways. How will you adjust, especially if you keep grieving the way things used to be? Just remember that I love all My children with their various styles of worship. I get a kick out of all the ways My kiddos lift their voices in praise. Hopefully, you will, too, in time. Don't be surprised if you see people worshipping with abandon, hands and arms raised in joyous praise. From heaven, those outstretched arms look beautiful to Me. Styles of worship are as individual as My children, so keep your heart and mind open. Perhaps you'll find yourself morphing and growing with your new church.

SHOCKING ACCIDENT

. . . .

*"I have said these things to you, that in me
you may have peace. In the world you will
have tribulation. But take heart;
I have overcome the world."*

JOHN 16:33 ESV

The unthinkable has happened. A tragic accident has altered your world. It's left you reeling. You're in shock. You're numb. You're unable to move to the right or left or to take a step forward. If only you could feel the world beneath your feet once again. Then, perhaps, things could go back to normal. Right now you're wondering if anything will ever be normal again. How can it be, after the shock you've been through? Oh, sweet daughter, how I long to bring stability, even now. I know it seems impossible, but I can steady your feet. I can add My salve to your fractured heart. And even though you are in the very middle of tribulation, you can come through it as strong as ever with My help. How do I know this? Because I've seen it time and time again throughout history. I think of the time I walked with David through the loss of his child. What brokenness he faced. And yet, I worked in his heart to bring healing. This is My plan. In every situation, I long to bring healing and perfect peace.

DISTANCE

. . . .

For though I am absent in body, yet I am with
you in spirit, rejoicing to see your good order
and the firmness of your faith in Christ.

COLOSSIANS 2:5 ESV

Distance. The word was never a problem before. But now that distance has grown between you and a loved one, and you ponder it daily. It's not like mileage on a map. The kind of distance you're dealing with is more of the "I wonder if they've forgotten I even exist?" variety or the "Why won't they let me see my grandchildren? I'm their grandmother, after all" sort. You wish things were different. You wish you could wipe away those imaginary miles and close the gap, to make things like they once were. Oh, dear girl, please let Me give you another word to contemplate: *close*. I'm as close as your next heartbeat. There are no miles between us, real or imagined. And I hope you already know that I'll never leave you or forsake you. This grief over distance has been very real to you (and I get it), but I will bring others into your life who will fill that gap very nicely. Hang in there. Stick close to Me. We'll get through this rough patch together.

Thy Will Be Done

. . . .

"Abba, Father," he said, "everything is possible for you. Take this cup from me. Yet not what I will, but what you will."

MARK 14:36 NIV

The four hardest words many of My children will ever utter: *Thy will be done.* You've had to speak it in so many different situations: When a parent faced a devastating diagnosis. When a child was emotionally wounded at school. When a friend turned on you. When you were forced to move due to a job situation. When the thing you'd prayed for didn't come to pass. And though those words haven't come easily, they've been music to My ears. Those four words are a sign that you are fully committed to My will in your life and the lives of those you care about. Putting them in My hands is the best thing you can do (though it might not always seem like it in the moment). You can trust Me. I have good things in store for you (and your loved ones). It's My good pleasure to take care of My children. So keep on saying it, sweet girl: "Thy will be done." You'll never be sorry you trusted Me. . .I promise.

THE TICKING CLOCK

. . . .

But do not overlook this one fact, beloved,
that with the Lord one day is as a thousand
years, and a thousand years as one day.

2 PETER 3:8 ESV

Time is racing by. Seems like just yesterday you were young. Opportunity ruled the day and happily-ever-afters were in every imagined thought. Now the clock is ticking and you wish you could turn back the hands of time. The children aren't tiny anymore. In fact, they're grown and gone. Your body is starting to show signs of aging. You're not a fan of the changes and would do anything to hit the REWIND button. Only there isn't a REWIND button. You've adopted the phrase "Getting old isn't for sissies." You're right. It's not. Life is a journey, daughter. It's a road filled with twists and turns, some of them tougher than others. There's no U-turn ahead to send you back to where you started. Every day is a gift, even those days that shine a spotlight on changes. And yes, the clock is ticking. But it's not ticking here, in heaven. In this glorious place there are no time constraints or woes. So set your eyes on heaven. But in the meantime, don't begrudge the days. See them as the gift they are—from Me to you.

The Resurrection and Life

....

*Jesus said to her, "I am the resurrection
and the life. The one who believes in me
will live, even though they die."*

JOHN 11:25 NIV

All you want to do is lie in bed with the covers pulled up
to your chin. There's no stirring you from your grief these
days. The life you once knew is gone, replaced with grief
and frustration. In your darkest moments you wonder if
you will ever walk among the living again. I want to remind
you of a promise from My Word: I am the resurrection.
That means I'm pretty good at raising people up from the
depths, the miry places. I can, with a touch of My hand,
raise you from the place of frozen grief. I am also the life.
That means I can regenerate and cause things to start
over. This might seem impossible to you in your current
situation, but I have the ability to stir you back to life, to
rouse you from that place you've been to a hopeful road
ahead. In order to receive these gifts, you must shift your
gaze. Look up, away from the pillow, away from the covers.
Look to Me. Ask for My resurrection power, then watch
as I perform on your behalf.

It Is Well with My Soul

*We have this hope as an anchor for the soul,
firm and secure. It enters the inner sanctuary
behind the curtain, where our forerunner,
Jesus, has entered on our behalf.*

HEBREWS 6:19–20 NIV

You've sung the words to the old hymn dozens of times. During the upbeat seasons, those words were easy to voice, weren't they? But what about now? Now, with the chaos, the pain, the grief, it's almost impossible to even whisper the words: "It is well with my soul." I understand. It doesn't feel well. It doesn't look well. In fact, you wonder if things will ever be well again. I understand, precious one, and I care. Part of the "wellness" journey includes trusting Me in the seasons that don't make sense. When you whisper the words "It is well with my soul," what you're really saying is, "I trust You, Lord. I trust You to somehow turn this devastating situation into something usable for the journey. I trust You to mend my broken heart and to restore what has been lost. I trust You to somehow restore my hope and my foundation so that I don't completely crumble." You can trust Me. When My will is done, restoration takes place. Empty places are filled. Hope is restored. Vision is recast. Can you whisper those words, even now? *"It is well with my soul."* Speak them, and watch Me move.

The Whole Armor

Finally, be strong in the Lord and in his mighty power. Put on the full armor of God, so that you can take your stand against the devil's schemes.

Ephesians 6:10–11 niv

You've felt defenseless. The attacks have come out of nowhere. They've nearly taken you down. You've felt the sting of arrows as they pierce your skin, and you've wondered why no one has stepped up to protect you. The grief over all of this is very real, very palpable. Oh, but grieve no longer! I'm here, daughter. I'm here to guard, to protect, and to surround you on every side, so that those arrows will whiz right by you and not hit their intended target. You have a very real enemy, and he's angry. He'll do anything to take you down. This is why I've given you My armor. Put it on daily. Put on that breastplate. Put on those shoes of peace. You can live your life fully covered, fully protected, taking a strong stand against the devil's schemes. Just let him try to shoot that next arrow at you. I'll send it sailing across the stratosphere, into the abyss where it belongs. You are My child, and I'm in protective dad–mode. No weapon formed against you will prosper. You can take that promise to the bank.

GOAL SETTING

. . . .

"For which one of you, when he wants to build a tower, does not first sit down and calculate the cost to see if he has enough to complete it?"

LUKE 14:28 NASB

You set goals. They seemed realistic, doable. You set out on the right path, convinced you'd meet every one with little or no real effort. But you didn't. In fact, you didn't even come close on a few. Maybe you overestimated your abilities? Maybe you were crazy to think you might make progress? So you gave up, convinced you didn't have what it took to get there. Today I'd like to reassure you that I can help with every goal you set. Sure, your goals need to be realistic, but don't be afraid to stretch yourself. With My help, you can go further than you think. So grab that laptop. Open that spreadsheet. Begin to think about where you want to be next year at this time. What about five years from now? How about ten years? How will you get there? It starts with a well-thought-out strategy. I'll help you with that part, too, if you'll let Me. Let's get busy, girl. We've got goals to set. . .and meet.

Refuge and Strength

. . . .

"The eternal God is your refuge, and underneath
are the everlasting arms. He will drive out your
enemies before you, saying, 'Destroy them!' "

DEUTERONOMY 33:27 NIV

You've known the pain and weariness of the battlefield.
You've felt it internally during this past season of your
life. Many days you've wanted to run to a place of safety
and shelter, to escape the madness of reality. If only you
had a physical place to hide, where you could recover,
where your body, heart, and mind would have a chance
to process what you've been through. You'd be there in a
heartbeat, I know. But there is no cabin in the woods, no
private island getaway. There is no recovery hospital where
medical personnel tend to your wounds. You sometimes
wonder if people even notice how badly wounded you are.
I would like to encourage you to run to Me. You won't find
Me in an actual place, because I'm everywhere; but you
will find a shelter from the storm. . .I promise. And I will
be your refuge, your protector, the One who guards and
keeps you. I'll hover over you and give you time to heal
from the inside out. Best of all, I will give you the strength
to face the future. So hide away with Me, daughter. Healing
takes time. We've got work to do.

A Very Present Help in Trouble

- -

God is our refuge and strength, a very present help in trouble. Therefore we will not fear, though the earth should change and though the mountains slip into the heart of the sea.

PSALM 46:1–2 NASB

You've always been the one to rush to everyone's defense. What a warrior you've been on behalf of those you love. Now you're wishing someone would run toward you. Where are the warriors when you need them? Instead, the battlefield is empty. You look around, waiting for someone to bring aid during this season when you've been so wounded, but there is no assistance. You've never felt more alone. And now you're grieving what feels like a total abandonment—from those you love and even from Me. Oh, My daughter, I am here. I am very present. That means I have borne witness to what you've endured, and I'm next to you, even now, to bring aid. I didn't have to rush in to your defense because I never left you in the first place. So I encourage you today to reconsider those feelings of aloneness. And while you're at it, release that fear to Me. I am a very present help in times of trouble.

SPEAK TO THE MOUNTAIN

. . . .

"Truly I tell you, if anyone says to this
mountain, 'Go, throw yourself into the sea,'
and does not doubt in their heart but believes
that what they say will happen,
it will be done for them."

MARK 11:23 NIV

Grief has caused your faith to wane. I understand. Distractions have risen like mountains in front of you, blocking your view and making small matters look huge. You used to be such a woman of faith, ready to speak to any mountain that dared to rise up in front of you. But the grief has changed you. It has robbed you of the very thing you need most right now. Your waning faith has affected many areas of your life. You're asking, "But how can I put my faith in You, Lord, when You've let me down?" Oh, sweet girl, I haven't let you down. I can't imagine hurting any of My children. I am not the source of your disappointment, though it may look that way. I'm in the business of "appointing," not "disappointing." So face those mountains with your shoulders squared. Garner the courage to speak to them with the expectation that I will move on your behalf as the very words flow forth from your lips. *Know* that it will happen. Truly *know* it in your heart. I promise that your faith will grow as you speak. Before long, you'll be known as a mountain mover, a true bulldozer in the faith.

Call Upon My Name

. . . .

*"Then you will call on me and come
and pray to me, and I will listen to you."*

JEREMIAH 29:12 NIV

Remember playing outside with your friends as a kid?
Your mama would call for you at suppertime. Even from
far off, you recognized her loving voice. Your name would
ring out across the open spaces, beckoning you to come
home—for dinner, for family time, for love and attention.
Oh, the rush of memories as you think about how you
felt as you bolted toward home. The same is still true as
I call out to you. Did you know that your name is always
on My lips? It's true. And guess what? I'd love it if My
name was always on your lips, too, especially when you're
going through a grieving season. When you take the time
to call out to Me, when you spend time in prayer, I will
hearken. That means I'll listen. No, I won't respond in the
same way your parents did around the dinner table, but
I'll whisper sweet words in your ear and encouragement to
your broken heart. So let's spend time together, shall we?

Binding Wounds

. . . .

He heals the brokenhearted
and binds up their wounds.

PSALM 147:3 NIV

I've been watching how you love others. You're an amazing caregiver to so many. Multiple times you've wrapped the wounds of others, even those who weren't particularly kind to you. What a wonderful and dedicated friend and family member you've been! Wrapping provides two answers to the problem: it shields the injury from infection and secures the area, adding strength. In many cases, binding up the wound is critical to the survival of the patient. Lately, you've felt like a patient yourself. The grieving has been something akin to an open wound, one that won't heal. And though you've tried to shore things up, to wrap and secure the issue, you're not getting any better. Will you trust Me to bind, child? I've got the ointment, the salve. I'll dress that broken heart and heal those fractured emotions. It will sting at first, in much the same way that a wound burns when you cleanse it, but it will be worth it, I promise. Cleansing will come. Healing will come. Hope will come. . .if you will allow Me to bind those wounds with My grace, My love, My care.

IGNORE THE LIES

. . . .

"The Rock! His work is perfect, for all His ways are just; a God of faithfulness and without injustice, righteous and upright is He."

DEUTERONOMY 32:4 NASB

❧

There's a reason My Word makes it clear that I hate lies. They always bring about destruction and pain. They are a direct tool of the enemy, meant to bring division and pain. He'll do anything to avoid the truth. Now you're in the line of fire. People have lied about you. They've made up stories that simply aren't true, or they've exaggerated tales to spread gossip. You're wounded by these lies, but how can truth be restored to the situation? Rest easy. That's where I come in. I'm a specialist in truth. And I alone can speak to the hearts of those who need to know it. So don't spend too many hours trying to vindicate yourself. Instead, wait for My intervention. I can do in a moment what you can't do in hours—and weeks—of trying. And don't hate the one who started the drama. It will only aggravate the situation if you give yourself over to bitterness. Instead, offer forgiveness, and watch as I sweep in and create order from chaos.

DEATH, WHERE IS THY STING?

. . . .

"Where, O death, is your victory?
Where, O death, is your sting?"

1 CORINTHIANS 15:55 NIV

For the unbeliever, death carries a true sting, an eternal one, no less. You've just come from a funeral. The one who passed away wasn't a believer. For days you've wondered how to control your emotions. If only you had done this, if only you had said that. But it's too late now, and you're grieving as a result. There's a weight, a heaviness, that comes with knowing the truth about eternity. It definitely stings to know that the person you cared about will be separated from Me in the afterlife. What can you do about it, though? Oh, My child, I long for you to do one thing and only one: live your life in such a way that others will come to know Me by your actions. Don't dwell on what has already transpired. Set your gaze forward. There will be many lives ahead, many people you've not even met yet who will have softened hearts. They will be watching your actions. They will be listening to your words. They will see you as a walking, talking Jesus, a true representation of what heaven looks like in earthly form. So don't let this sting last for long. We have work to do. Let's get to it.

AUTOPILOT

* *

My comfort in my suffering is this:
your promise preserves my life.

PSALM 119:50 NIV

You've been living on autopilot. You're still functioning (physically) but have emotionally checked out. The plane is flying on its own without your input. Your daily life consists of lugging from place to place, doing things from rote. But your heart just isn't in it. Not anymore. The grief has dragged you to a different place, one where numbness rules the day and joy is zapped. I can help you transition out of this place. With My help, you can take the gears once again and see beyond the windshield of your life with clarity and hopefulness. It's going to require courage, but I know you. (In fact, I know you better than anyone else does.) You've got it in you. I know, because I put it there. The journey will begin with a change of vision. Take a good, long look out of the windshield. See those pretty white clouds? See that blue sky? It's beckoning you to live again, to find joy again, to redirect your thinking. Set your gaze on the future. It's bright. It's sunny. It's filled with moments of joy and grace. We'll get there together, My hand atop yours on the gears. Together, we'll soar above the circumstances and experience new heights.

CATASTROPHE

The L͟O͟R͟D͟ gives strength to his people;
the L͟O͟R͟D͟ blesses his people with peace.

PSALM 29:11 NIV

Seems like every day you turn on the news and hear of another catastrophe: Terrorist attack. Earthquake. Stock market crash. Horrific accident. Incoming storm. These catastrophes are the headline stories, spreading fear and panic. Folks in the media capitalize on it. Anything to improve TV ratings. They seem to thrive on the drama. But I don't. Instead of stirring up panic and strife, I want to bring peace in the middle of these terrible times. I want to remind My children (all of them covering the globe) that I'm bigger than any catastrophe they could face. I'm bigger than that hurricane. I'm bigger than the financial losses. I'm bigger than the hole in your heart after losing a loved one in a catastrophic event. And I'm as steady as a rock, even when things are whirling out of control around you. So don't let the catastrophes shake you too badly. Cling tight to Me. And don't hyperfocus on what you see or hear on television. You'll get overly anxious if you do. I'm the One to watch. I'm the One to listen to. I'm the One who will hold you, secure you, and protect you every step of the way.

Yahweh-Shalom

*And Gideon built an altar to the LORD there
and named it Yahweh-Shalom (which means
"the LORD is peace"). The altar remains
in Ophrah in the land of the clan
of Abiezer to this day.*

JUDGES 6:24 NLT

In the old days, My people would build an altar at each memorable place so that they would never forget the miracle I performed for them there. Oh, how I wish My children would still take the time to do this. There would be many altars in your life journey. Remember that time I healed you? And what about that moment when I rescued you from danger? Remember that day when your child was facing a devastating situation and I intervened? Those were "altar-building" moments. Why is it important to build an altar? Because these are the places where I brought peace in the middle of chaos. This is what I specialize in, by the way. I long to bring peace. One of My many names is Yahweh-Shalom (the Lord is peace). Even in the midst of your deepest grief, I'm Yahweh-Shalom. When you're facing bankruptcy, I'm Yahweh-Shalom. When your elderly parent is losing the ability to remember even the simplest of things, I'm Yahweh-Shalom. I'll bring peace to every situation you invite Me into, and before you know it, you'll have altars of remembrance all over the place.

ACCORDING TO MY WORD

My soul is weary with sorrow;
strengthen me according to your word.

PSALM 119:28 NIV

According to My Word. That's how I do things. And I love it
when My kids say things like, "Heal me according to Your
Word," or "Increase my joy according to Your Word," or
even "Help me, Lord, according to Your Word." Why add
the "according to Your Word" part? Because everything
you need for daily living, everything you need to overcome
the hurdles, everything you need to heal from the pain of
grief—it's all covered in My Word. There's not one issue
you'll face, one valley you'll walk through, one heartache
you'll experience that's not covered in My Word. The Bible
is complete in that it offers a cure for whatever ails you.
So use it in that way. Expect to find the answers within
its pages. Open it with the sense that I've got the cure.
Even in your darkest hour I'll illuminate the passages you
need to bring hope and life. Best of all, My Word (tried
and true through the ages) brings comfort and strength. It
will remind you that I had a plan for your life long before
you even arrived on the planet.

OVERCOME THE WORLD

. . . .

*"I have told you these things, so that in me
you may have peace. In this world you
will have trouble. But take heart!
I have overcome the world."*

JOHN 16:33 NIV

"In this world you will have trouble." Oh, how you'd like to remove those words from your vocabulary. If only the world didn't have tribulation. If only the blissful state from the garden of Eden still remained. Wouldn't things be easier? The truth is, you are living in a fallen world. It wasn't My plan for sin to enter in, trust Me. I would have preferred that My children walk in obedience and ease all of their days. But things went a different direction in the garden (a direct result of free will merged with temptation), and you're seeing the results in this broken world in which you live. That's why it's more important than ever to realize that I truly have overcome the world. You might be in it, but you're certainly not of it. And if I'm the Overcomer, then you (My child) are an overcomer, too. That should give you plenty of reason to take heart. No matter what you go through, you can (and will) overcome. Why am I telling you this today of all days? So that you may have peace.

Open Ears

The eyes of the LORD are toward the righteous
and His ears are open to their cry. . . .
The righteous cry, and the LORD hears
and delivers them out of all their troubles.

PSALM 34:15, 17 NASB

You've been in this situation before: You're carrying on a conversation with a friend, a loved one, a child. . .and it's obvious they're not hearing a word you're saying. Oh, they're nodding. They're playing along. But they're not really paying full attention. Their eyes have shifted. They're not giving full responses. They look bored. They're not engaged. That's how I feel sometimes when I'm talking to My children. They're going to church. Facing forward as the pastor preaches. But they're already thinking about their plans for the week or where they'll eat lunch. They're not really engaged in the process. I want you to know that I'll never do that to you. When you talk to Me, I'm here for you. I'm not just looking at you, nodding. I'm taking in every word. I'm listening to the intonations. And I care deeply. Nothing matters more to Me in this moment (especially when you're hurting) than you. There's nothing to distract Me from the one I love. I promise. So gaze into My eyes. I'm right here, ready to listen.

BE STILL AND KNOW

*He says, "Be still, and know that I am
God; I will be exalted among the nations,
I will be exalted in the earth."*

PSALM 46:10 NIV

You're kicking yourself. You can't go back and change anything, but you wish you could. If only you had been there. You could have prevented the tragedy. If only you had spoken a word of warning, the crisis could have been averted. If only, if only. Your heart is overwhelmed with if-onlys. Child, today I'm going to ask you to be still and know that I am God. I know all. I see all. And I need you to know in your heart of hearts that the if-onlys will only make things worse. There's no room for questioning yourself now. Yes, there are lessons to be learned, but beating yourself up won't help anything. In fact, it will stop you in your tracks. Can you trust Me with the if-onlys? I want to ease your conscience and restore your ability to breathe without pain. I want to see you freed up so that you can regain your effectiveness. Most of all, I want to comfort you in your time of grief and show you that life will go on. There are still memories to be made, people to be loved, and joys to be had. Be still, and let Me convince you in a way that only I can.

THE ROCK THAT IS HIGHER

. . . .

From the ends of the earth I call to you,
I call as my heart grows faint; lead me to
the rock that is higher than I.

PSALM 61:2 NIV

You've worked for months to prove yourself. You've done everything a person could do to show your boss that you've got the goods. But you didn't get the raise. You didn't get the promotion. You didn't even get a nod or an attagirl. You're struggling with anger, which is grief's way of boiling to the surface. It's not fair. It's beyond not fair. Trust Me when I say that I understand the word *unfair*. I could argue that it wasn't fair that I had to go to the cross to pay the price for your sins. I could debate that it wasn't fair to remain in the grave for three days before rising again. So many things in life don't seem fair; but remember, there is always a greater plan at work. The promotion you didn't get today? It could free you up to get something better later on. That raise you were hoping for but didn't receive? I'll bring provision some other way, I promise. Look for Me to surprise you. The point is, I see those unfair things you're wrestling with from a slightly different perspective. If only you had My vision. Then you could realize that I'm truly up to something here.

A STRONG TOWER

The name of the LORD is a strong tower;
the righteous run to it and are safe.

PROVERBS 18:10 NKJV

I see your tears in the night. I hear your cries. So many unfulfilled dreams, things that never came to pass. You don't think about them during the daylight hours; but at night, when things finally slow down, you grieve the things that might have been. *Should* have been (at least to your way of thinking). You try to rewrite history in your mind and wish you really could go back for a few do-overs. But that's not part of My plan. Instead of seeing Me as a dream crusher, I hope you will begin to look at Me as a strong tower. I'm the place you run to when you're feeling hurt (like now). I'm the safe place, the One you can tell your troubles to. I'm here to mend that heart when dreams are unfulfilled, and I'm here to whisper, "There are plenty of dreams ahead," when you get discouraged. My purpose as a tower is to be strong when you are not. So what are you waiting for? Bring those broken dreams. Come with that fractured heart. Rush to the tower, where you will find healing and hope once more.

CARING FOR OTHERS

*Surely he took up our pain and bore our suffering,
yet we considered him punished by God,
stricken by him, and afflicted. But he was pierced
for our transgressions, he was crushed for our
iniquities; the punishment that brought us peace
was on him, and by his wounds we are healed.*

ISAIAH 53:4–5 NIV

You're a wonderful caregiver. Your hours of service to your loved one haven't gone unnoticed, at least not by Me. But you're wearing yourself out. You've paid a lot of attention to the needs of your patient but not yourself. It's time to adjust your schedule, to work in some "you" time. Where should you start? In My Word. It's loaded with all sorts of verses and stories to inspire you. You'll find instruction for the days ahead, but you'll also find comfort for where you are right now. I see that you're struggling. I realize you're feeling alone. But My Word will give you everything you need in every moment. Your emotional health is as important to Me as your physical health, so begin to focus on your own needs. Get some rest. Delegate. Find easier ways to accomplish tasks. Most of all, lay your burdens at My feet. You're not meant to carry this alone. I'm right here. I took the pain. I bore the sorrow. By My wounds, every emotional need you could ever have is already met. That's how much I adore you.

At Home with the Lord

· ·

*We are of good courage, I say,
and prefer rather to be absent from the body
and to be at home with the Lord.*

2 Corinthians 5:8 NASB

The house feels empty. You walk from room to room, looking at the furniture, the pictures on the wall, the little knickknacks. The things are all still there, but the hollow echoes down the hallway as you speak are a reminder that one you loved is now gone. You would do anything to bring your loved one back, but it's impossible. So the home itself becomes a tomb, and you bury yourself in it, unable to function outside its walls. It's a conundrum, really. The very house that brings you pain is where you plant yourself. Your friends are beginning to worry. Your family has already expressed concern. But you refuse to budge. Oh, sweet daughter, I created you to live. Yes, you're grieving. Yes, you've discovered it's easier to stay locked up inside the house where the memories are. But feeling at home isn't so much about a physical place. I want you to be at home with Me. In fact, I'd love it if you would take that grief you're feeling and let Me help you through it. Today, make an effort to step outside that front door. Go someplace different. Meet Me in the park or at the library. Visit with Me at the mall or in the grocery store. But take several steps away from the house. There's life outside those four walls, I promise.

ENTREPRENEURIAL GRIEF

. . . .

"Love your enemies, do good to those who hate you, bless those who curse you, pray for those who mistreat you. If someone slaps you on one cheek, turn to them the other also. If someone takes your coat, do not withhold your shirt from them. Give to everyone who asks you, and if anyone takes what belongs to you, do not demand it back."

LUKE 6:27–30 NIV

You worked for years to build your company. Not one detail was overlooked. You sought out the very best partner and felt secure when you found one. The partnership worked like a charm. . .until it didn't. Putting your finger on what went wrong has been tough. I've seen you struggle through this. And the eventual loss of the business? I see how that broke your heart and left you feeling confused and angry. Being pushed out by your partner made no sense. Your work, your pay, your future, your desires. . .all down the tubes. And now you're grieving as if you'd lost a loved one. My heart is with you. And even though people may stab you in the back, I never will. I won't steal from you or nudge you out. We're in the kind of partnership that will last throughout eternity. In other words, you can trust Me. So let's begin to build on this relationship. I'm going to prepare you for that next big thing, and I promise you won't be disappointed by the work I will do inside your heart.

SURRENDERING YOUR
CHILD TO GOD

. . . .

*He said to them, "Go into all the world
and preach the gospel to all creation."*

MARK 16:15 NIV

She's doing exactly what you'd always hoped and prayed
she would do: she's giving herself to Me. That daughter
of yours has fallen in love with Me (and My people) and
has decided to offer her life in service on the mission
field. What a proud parent you are. Still, you're grieving
a little on the inside. A big move is in her future. She's
headed to unknown places, to take on big tasks. And
though you're proud of her, you're also terrified. Will she
be safe? How will you handle life at home without her?
What if she leaves and never comes back? Will she adapt
so fully to her new home, her new culture, that she forgets
where she came from? Oh, sweet child, how I wish you
could see her through My eyes. What a lovely perspective!
I've whispered sweet words into her ear, and she's not
only listened but responded. I told her to "Go" and she's
going! What blissful obedience! You can trust her in My
care, I promise. I'll shelter her on every side. And don't
worry about "losing her." She's still your girl. She'll stay in
touch. You raised her right, Mama. So settle that heart.
I have a few things I need to whisper to you as well. And
who knows? . . . You might just be setting out on a few
adventures of your own.

Separation Due to Addiction

It is for freedom that Christ has set us free.
Stand firm, then, and do not let yourselves
be burdened again by a yoke of slavery.

Galatians 5:1 niv

Addiction. What a horrible word. You never thought you'd have to speak this ugly word, let alone live with its consequences. And yet, someone you love is caught in the tentacles of addiction and can't seem to break free. You've tried everything to help: interventions, words of wisdom, prayer, strategies for freedom. Still the addiction remains. And because it remains, you've had to make a hard choice, one that has left you grieving. You've had to break ties. Tough love is now the rule of the day. It's for the best—for everyone—but you find yourself doubting the decision. As much as you long for freedom for your loved one, I ache for it even more. I admire your tough-love stance. It's a form of protection, keeping you from being drawn into the drama. I want your loved one's full attention, and he can't see his need if you're constantly rescuing. So take a step back. It's okay. I'll take it from here. And don't grieve. Instead, begin to celebrate the recovery that will come once freedom from this addiction takes place. It's more than possible with My kind of intervention.

LOSS OF SAVINGS

The LORD is my shepherd,
I lack nothing.

PSALM 23:1 NIV

Your little nest egg has been robbed. You never saw it coming. An unexpected medical expense zapped you of every spare cent and then some. The bills keep flooding in, but you're out of options. Should you rob Peter to pay Paul? Will there be consequences if you do? None of this feels fair. You worked so hard to save for a rainy day. Now it's pouring outside, and there's no money left to tend to the things that matter. You've given it all away to something that just feels unnecessary, something you didn't plan for. The loss of this saved income has devastated you and caused you to lose hope. How can you possibly begin again? Look to Me, child. I am your provider. I saw this situation coming, and I've already made provision for it. You did a great job of saving. You were responsible and obedient. But I have other ways of bringing in funds, ways that might just surprise you. Yes, this is a hard season, but I have a plan, even now. You can still trust Me, even when the bank account is sitting on empty.

LOSS OF SEXUALITY

So Boaz took Ruth
and she became his wife.

Your marriage has been a beautiful gift. You're paired with just the right partner, one who has adored you for years. The intimate relations you've shared throughout the marriage have been so sweet. But lately, things are changing. The "togetherness" part has been lacking. Your feelings about your sexuality have been shifting as you've aged, and it's affecting your intimate life. These changes are normal, daughter, but I want you to be on the lookout for the enemy's schemes. He would love to separate you from your spouse, not just physically but emotionally as well. Once those feelings of separation come, they're hard to counter. My goal is to bring unity, both in the natural and in the spiritual. I want to bring wholeness to your one-flesh union. While I'm at work in this area, stay open to the idea. I'll take you back to the early days of cuddling and teasing, sweetness and flirting. If you'll let Me. Watch Me as I work to restore what the enemy has attempted to steal. Intimacy, you see, is far more than sexual. I'm about to surprise you with new ideas for keeping that marriage healthy and strong.

LACK OF CLOSENESS
WITH GROWN CHILD

*As a prisoner for the Lord, then, I urge you
to live a life worthy of the calling you have
received. Be completely humble and gentle;
be patient, bearing with one another in love.
Make every effort to keep the unity of
the Spirit through the bond of peace.*

EPHESIANS 4:1–3 NIV

He's busy. You're busy. Life is crazy, hectic. The days pass in a blur, and the lack of communication feels normal. After a while, you almost forget to be sad that the relationship is fading. And then something happens to remind you: A picture from the past. A song he used to love. A phrase he used to use. In that moment you're reminded afresh of how sweet things used to be before busyness intervened. But how can you get back to the way things were? Will you ever be close again? Oh, My child, I'll help. It starts with a kind word. A sweet text. A phone call. Nothing big. Nothing demanding. Just a sweet "Great to talk to you" moment. I'll take it from there. I can, in a moment, flood that loved one's heart with sweet emotions, good memories, and a desire to draw close once again. So don't nag. Don't push. And most of all, don't fret. If you will allow Me to take charge, I promise you'll be tickled with the results.

My Side, Your Side

. . . .

But God has put the body together,
giving greater honor to the parts that lacked it,
so that there should be no division in the
body, but that its parts should have
equal concern for each other.

1 Corinthians 12:24–25 niv

You never saw this coming. The family, once united, has now split down the middle. A divorce has caused people to take sides. Folks you once trusted with your life are now defensive and angry. They're not speaking to one another. One or two have even turned on you, as if you somehow caused this. You're caught in the fray, unsure of how to respond. After all, you love all these people. You don't want to take sides. I appreciate this response on your end. I don't like division either. I've never been one for splitting up families or taking sides. So what's your role in this situation? Love them. All of them. Love the ones who are causing trouble. Love those who've been hurt. Love the ones who are angry and defensive. Move with great caution so as not to further stir the pot, but don't be afraid to love. And pray. Leave these folks in My capable hands and let Me do the necessary work. It might not look pretty in the moment, but I promise I can make something beautiful out of this mess.

FEAR OF LOSS
(WHEN THINGS ARE GOING WELL)

. . . .

But Jesus spoke to them at once.
"Don't be afraid," he said.
"Take courage. I am here!"

MATTHEW 14:27 NLT

You've always been a glass-half-full kind of person. Until lately. Loss after loss has left you with a more pessimistic view. Every time you come up for air, something else happens. Now the waters have calmed. No tragedies of late. But you're still waiting for the other shoe to drop. You can't relax and enjoy the peaceful moments because you're jaded by the pain. It's bound to strike again. Right? Isn't that how it works? Just about the time you think you're safe. . .*bam!* Oh, how I wish you could relax and enjoy the moment. Let Me work on your perspective so that you can settle into this season and receive the necessary healing to move forward. And no, I'm not out to get you. It doesn't work like that, though circumstances might convince you otherwise. I adore you. I'm not here to bring pain. I'm the Great Restorer. You can trust Me. If you could see what's going on behind the scenes, you'd see all the shoes I've kept from dropping. That would help you put things in perspective.

The Shadow of My Wings

He will cover you with his feathers, and under his wings you will find refuge; his faithfulness will be your shield and rampart.

PSALM 91:4 NIV

Refuge. Isn't that a lovely word? Lately, you've needed a refuge (a shelter) from the many storms in your life. They've flooded over you, blinding you and causing you to lose your way. You haven't known where to run. The people you've always run to in the past seemed to be getting weary with your downcast face and overwhelmed state of mind. The job? Sure, it keeps you busy, but you can't avoid the obvious forever. And yes, you've even run to food. I've seen it, and your body is starting to show the effects of it. I have the perfect solution, child. Run to Me and watch as I cover you. I will provide the refuge you need. I'll be your shelter from the storm, your shield of protection. You won't have to look for these things from people anymore. Or from busyness. Or from food. All you need is found in Me. I want to be your shelter. Will you let Me? My arms are wide open. Let Me cover you until the storm passes.

Rebounding from Remission

Joy is gone from our hearts;
our dancing has turned to mourning.

LAMENTATIONS 5:15 NIV

Remission. How you loved hearing that word. You celebrated with full abandon, convinced the journey (at least the bad parts) was behind you. Now you've received word that the disease has manifested again. You're in shock. This wasn't supposed to happen. News of your remission had allowed you to hope again, to see the future as a bright and shiny place. Now you're left confused, angry, and terrified. The return of the disease has brought about a hopelessness that you can't conquer on your own. That's why I want you to look solely to Me. I'm still here. This shocking news has shaken you to the core, but I'm standing as solid as a rock. I will not be moved, no matter the diagnosis. And I want to prove, once and for all, that I'm here *with* you and *for* you. I plan to breathe peace into that fear. I plan to speak life over death. I plan to whisper, "You can do this," when you feel you can't go on. We will walk hand in hand through this. If you draw close, I will use this next season of your life as our closest yet. Breathe deep, daughter. We've got this.

Grieving Food (While Dieting)

*And after you have suffered a little while,
the God of all grace, who has called you to
his eternal glory in Christ, will himself restore,
confirm, strengthen, and establish you.*

1 Peter 5:10 esv

Cheesecake. Pasta. Garlic bread. You want it. All of it. But it's not yours for the taking, at least not at the moment. You're in a season of lifestyle changes, and those things are off your plate. Literally. It doesn't seem fair. Your friends? They're eating whatever they want. They're not slaving at the gym. They don't gain five pounds by looking at a banana split. Remember, daughter, this is your journey, not theirs. And I'm here to guide you as you make those necessary changes. It's not easy to lay down some of the foods you love, but I'll show you some healthier options and even tweak your taste buds to help you crave the good stuff. So don't grieve the sweets. Don't grieve the carbs. Shift your thoughts to how good it will feel to wear that dress you've had in the back of your closet for so long. Think about how wonderful it will be to travel without having to worry about fitting into the airplane seat. In other words, think about the future. Picture yourself—your *healthier* self—doing things you only dreamed of. It's all possible, if you just stick with it.

Grieving the "No" Answer

· ·

David praised the LORD in the presence of
the whole assembly, saying, "Praise be to you,
LORD, the God of our father Israel,
from everlasting to everlasting. Yours, LORD,
is the greatness and the power and the glory and
the majesty and the splendor, for everything in
heaven and earth is yours. Yours, LORD,
is the kingdom; you are exalted as head over all."

1 Chronicles 29:10–11 niv

I don't always answer with a yes. Many times you've asked, and I've come back with a firm no. You're not crazy about the "no" responses, but I want to assure you that I'm saying no for your own good. When I say no to today's requests, I'll be free to say yes to tomorrow's. In other words, there are better things ahead. I know, I know. . .you don't see it. You wanted a quick yes because you felt sure you'd asked for the better thing. Oh, if only you could see as I do. Then you would know without a doubt that what's coming is far greater than what you longed for. Sure, it's hard to give up on a dream or an idea, but what if My dream for you far surpasses what you had in mind? (Isn't that a lovely thought?) Don't grieve the nos, child. They're a passageway to some fantastic things ahead.

LOSS OF ATHLETICISM

When he has done this, then the Son himself will be made subject to him who put everything under him, so that God may be all in all.

1 CORINTHIANS 15:28 NIV

You used to be the athletic one. You could run faster than most or play harder than most. You took pride in your physique and in your ability to conquer a variety of sports. Now those abilities are waning. You find yourself struggling. You watch others participate in sporting events and grieve the old you, the one who could perform. Your body seems to be betraying you. You've never been one to sit on the sidelines, but what else can you do? Participation is a thing of the past. Oh, but it isn't! There are so many ways you can still play a role in the sports you love. Celebrate the athletes. Write articles about them. Send them notes of encouragement. Support a local team. Provide uniforms. Help them raise funds. There are a thousand different ways to stay active in the sports you love, even if your body won't allow you to play the game. You'll never have to sit on the sidelines again if you'll listen to My ideas. Together, we'll make a difference while keeping that smile on your face.

LOSS OF A SENTIMENTAL OBJECT

. . . .

Remember me, O my God, concerning this,
and do not wipe out my good deeds that I have
done for the house of my God and for his service.

NEHEMIAH 13:14 ESV

You've searched everywhere for it. Under the cushions. In every drawer. In the lockbox. Under the bed. But you can't find it. That sentimental item you'd planned to keep forever, the one that reminds you of that special person. . .it's gone. You've torn up the house, determined it will surface, but so far it has not. The idea of losing it grieves you. This item was a tangible link to the person you've lost. Now it's gone, and your heart is completely broken all over again. Give this grief to Me, child. I know what you're really struggling with—the physical link to your loved one. But I will keep your memories fresh if you will let Me. Use this opportunity to write down the things you loved about the person and about that treasured item you've lost. Write it all down so that you never forget, so that you can pass on the legacy. The written story will be sufficient to keep the memory alive and, unlike the keepsake, can be shared among all your family members. Everyone who knew and loved her will be reminded of the good times as they read what you've written. So don't grieve the tangible. Celebrate through story.

Grieving the Diagnosis

. . . .

But he was pierced for our transgressions,
he was crushed for our iniquities; the punishment
that brought us peace was on him, and by his
wounds we are healed.

Isaiah 53:5 niv

The doctor's report is in. You've been given a diagnosis. You knew it was coming—at least, you thought it might be coming—but now you're frozen in place by the words the physician has spoken. You're trying to process. The Internet is your new best friend. You type in the words over and over again, searching for articles, testimonies, stories of healing. . .anything. I understand the fear, daughter. It's a natural human emotion. This diagnosis was hard to hear and will be tough to walk through. But remember, those frightening words spoken by the doctor did not come as a surprise to Me. I'm still here, seated on My throne. Nothing about Me has changed. My promises today are as true as ever. Yes, you will grieve during the diagnosis phase, but don't stay in that place. In order for your body to heal you'll need to maintain a positive outlook. That begins by placing your hand in Mine. I'll teach you how to walk this road. At times I'll carry you. But I can promise you this—you'll never go it alone.

NEW FAMILY MEMBER

Love is patient, love is kind. It always protects, always trusts, always hopes, always perseveres.

1 CORINTHIANS 13:4, 7 NIV

You want to like her. She's new to the family, after all. But she's taking the place of someone you lost, and the idea makes you feel sick inside. Maybe you'll get used to her in time, but right now she feels like an outsider, an interloper. You're doing your best to include her, but it's hard. Everything inside of you wants to rebel, to kick her out, to go back to the way things used to be. Sweet daughter, I understand. My entire family is made up of outsiders, people who once didn't belong. But the wonderful thing about families is that they are meant to be inclusive. So exhibit some patience and kindness. Don't dishonor the newbie. Protect the family as a whole by protecting her as she eases her way in. Offer love, even if others don't. Include her as much as you are able. And above all, seek My answers to any emotions you might be facing during this season. I care, and I will show you how to make this journey in a way that will bring unity to your family.

REST FROM STRIVING

. . . .

*So there remains a Sabbath rest for the people
of God. For the one who has entered His
rest has himself also rested from his works,
as God did from His.*

HEBREWS 4:9–10 NASB

You're worn out. The situations in your life are exhausting, and all the stress is catching up with you. Even the so-called easy days aren't so easy. They're riddled with memories, emotions, and gut-wrenching reflection of what could have been. This season in particular has zapped you to the core. Grief wears the human body (and soul) out. And avoiding the grief? That will make you physically ill. So let it out, but guard yourself in the process. This starts with grieving My way. I want to provide you rest from the striving. Stop trying to figure things out. Stop trying to make things right. Stop replaying the tapes in your head so that you can change the outcome. Just rest. And My kind of rest (Sabbath rest) means you're not just crawling under the covers for a nap. I want to give you a deep-seated rest—one that can't be measured in hours or days. May your mind be at rest. May your heart be at rest. May your body be at rest. I'm working on a long-term healing plan for you, not just a quick fix. So grab those pajamas. We're about to get busy. . .resting.

GRIEVING THE PAIN YOU CAUSED

. . . .

*Do not lie to one another, since you laid aside
the old self with its evil practices, and have put
on the new self who is being renewed to
a true knowledge according to the image
of the One who created him.*

COLOSSIANS 3:9–10 NASB

You're not the same person you used to be. You don't do the same things. You don't hang out with the same people. The activities that used to be fun are fun no longer. Since you entered into a relationship with Me all that has changed. Your heart is different. But I see you struggling. You're looking backward at all the pain you caused others during the years before you met Me, and you're grieving. You left quite a trail. Lives were affected. Back then you didn't really care, but now? Well, now you wish you could undo all of it, go back and do things the right way. Maybe then people would still speak to you. Maybe then things would be different. I would encourage you to start this journey by thanking Me for saving you from the pit. I loved every second of giving you a second chance. Then pray for those you've hurt. Genuinely pray for them. I'll give you creative ways to offer apologies and to let them know that you've changed. Don't rush this process, or things will not end well. Trust My timing. I've got this.

PERSONALITY CHANGES

We pray this so that the name of our Lord Jesus may be glorified in you, and you in him, according to the grace of our God and the Lord Jesus Christ.

2 THESSALONIANS 1:12 NIV

You're usually pretty easygoing. Things don't get to you. But lately, since the grieving started, your personality has changed. You've developed a bit of a temper. You're more impatient with people. Worst of all, your perspective has shifted (you're seeing things in a more negative light), which has your actions a bit skewed. You never used to overreact to things, but now you do. People are noticing the changes, and they're commenting. Your knee-jerk reactions to their words have also been a little exaggerated. I've been watching all of this, and I can see that you're struggling. How you wish you could go back to the old you, the one who wasn't jaded. But you feel stuck. I will help you restore the joy the enemy has tried to steal. When that joy returns, you'll see a shift back to your old self. He's working overtime to rob you of the real you, but we're not going to let him. It's okay to grieve. Get it out. But don't let it create a monster. Focus on rebounding. Set your eyes on Me. We've got some work to do, but I'll accomplish it with love, grace, and a hefty dose of kindness.

LAZARUS, COME FORTH!

Mary. . .fell at His feet, saying to Him, "Lord, if You had been here, my brother would not have died." When Jesus therefore saw her weeping. . .He was deeply moved in spirit and was troubled, and said, "Where have you laid him?" They said to Him, "Lord, come and see." Jesus wept. So the Jews were saying, "See how He loved him!" But some of them said, "Could not this man, who opened the eyes of the blind man, have kept this man also from dying?"

JOHN 11:32–37 NASB

It's the shortest verse in the Bible, so short you might have buzzed right over it without seeing it. The words *Jesus wept* are in there for a reason. I had a good, long cry when Lazarus passed away. I'd lost a good friend, of course. I knew he would live again in eternity, but I missed him. I also grieved because I could see that people just weren't getting it. They didn't understand My message about eternity. Today, as you grieve that terrible loss, just know that I understand. I agonized in the garden of Gethsemene. I cried over Lazarus. I felt the same emotions you're now feeling. I am a God who gets it. And because I get it, I will work hard to make sure you make it through this season, triumphant.

PARENTAL WOES

For this reason his parents said,
"He is of age; ask him."

JOHN 9:23 NASB

You don't mind admitting it: You weren't the best parent. You messed up some things. In fact, you messed up a lot of things. The results are obvious when you look at your grown children. They have some issues. And while you can't pin them all on yourself, you do see shortcomings that can be traced back to your parenting. Is it too late to redeem these situations? What can you possibly do now? This would be a good time to remind you that parenting doesn't really end at age eighteen, like society would tell you. You are a parent all of your child's life. And while you can't give instruction in the same way, you can speak words of life and encouragement, no matter your age (or theirs). Spend time with Me. Get My perspective. I'll show you how to handle each grown child individually. The same growth you've seen in your life? You can see it in theirs. After all, I love them even more than you do and want to see them live their lives to the fullest. No nagging, Mom. No pressure. Just a plan of action to rework some of the problem spots. And while you're at it, don't beat yourself up. Most of the time you did the best you could do, working with the knowledge you had. Now that you've added Me to the team, we're going to see a more positive outcome.

LOSS OF TALENT

When he has done this, then the Son himself
will be made subject to him who put everything
under him, so that God may be all in all.

1 CORINTHIANS 15:28 NIV

Oh, what fun you had, sharing your talent. Everyone raved over your ability, your gift. It flowed like water pouring out of you, a true blessing to others and yourself. I gave you that gift, and I watched you develop it, nurture it, and use it to the best of your ability. What joy to watch you in your element, sharing from your heart. Talk about passionate! Talk about freeing! Your gift led the way and opened doors. Lately, though, you feel like that talent is waning. You're not as on point as you used to be. It doesn't come as naturally. In some ways, it feels as if I'm taking it away. I would never rob you of something that brings you joy. I do, however, allow you to walk through a variety of seasons, all different from each other, so that we can draw closer. Have you considered the fact that there are other gifts to be developed? There are doors you've not yet opened. Instead of grieving the loss of one talent, let's spend the next season developing another. And then another. I want you to be effective right here, right now. There are gifts aplenty just waiting. Let's get busy developing them.

A RARE DIAGNOSIS

Jesus was going through all the cities and villages, teaching in their synagogues and proclaiming the gospel of the kingdom, and healing every kind of disease and every kind of sickness.

MATTHEW 9:35 NASB

The diagnosis is in. The results: rare. You've got an unusual problem, one that most doctors don't know how to deal with. In fact, some don't even believe it to be a problem at all. You're tired of searching for answers and, harder still, tired of not being believed. You want to feel better, that's all. Forget the diagnosis. You just want life to go back to normal, for the symptoms to go away. And you want someone to take you seriously. You're weary of the raised eyebrows from folks in the medical community. I understand. People had a hard time believing Me, too. Folks always seem to want to hear the easy stuff, not the complex. But I've heard every word you've spoken, and I care. In fact, I care so much that I carried your sins to the cross. I took those stripes for your sake. I gave My life to bring you life. The work has already been done. So listen to the medical advice. But listen to My thoughts, too. My plan to bring about healing has already begun, after all.

Separation from Grandchildren

. . . .

" *'Do not fear, for I am with you; do not anxiously look about you, for I am your God. I will strengthen you'* "

ISAIAH 41:10 NASB

Their photos hang on your wall; their coloring pages are stuck with magnets to your refrigerator. You mail birthday presents from state to state. Their little voices greet you by phone whenever life slows down enough to allow a call. But you rarely get to see them in person. Other grandparents are posting on social media. They're taking their grandbabies to the children's museum, the movies, out to eat. You? You're secretly envious because you aren't able to do the same. In fact, you wonder if you'll ever have adequate time with those you love. Instead of grieving the distance, I have some creative ideas for you. Start a memory book for each long-distance grandchild. Fill it with photos as the years go by. And why not do a back-and-forth story? You start it with a paragraph then let your grandchild add the next. You will add the third paragraph and then return it to the child for another. Soon the two of you will have written a lovely tale. There are all sorts of long-distance activities you can do. Let's sit awhile and dream up a few ideas. Before long, you'll be excited about the possibilities, and all grieving will be behind you.

CLEAR THINKING

. . . .

And do not be conformed to this world,
but be transformed by the renewing of your mind,
so that you may prove what the will of God is,
that which is good and acceptable and perfect.

ROMANS 12:2 NASB

You've never been one to struggle with decision-making. In fact, you've been quick on the draw, able to see with clarity things that others couldn't see. Some would say you were the sharpest tool in the shed. But now things are different. Your vision is clouded. Your thoughts are muddy. Grief has added an extra layer of texture to the lens of your spiritual eyes, and you can't make out the road ahead the way you used to. And making decisions? Now? Impossible. Nothing looks doable to you. You try, but in the end you want to pull the covers over your head and simply ignore problems and everyday tasks. Oh, how I long to clear the lens. I'm in the vision business, dear one. I can remove the murky filter. I can bring clarity once again. Will you trust Me to remove the sticky layer of film from your thought life? Can I transform you once again? If so, you'll need to be ready to renew your mind (let Me make all things new). When we cross this bridge, I'll be able to show you My good and perfect will for your life.

LOSS OF AN ABUSIVE PARENT

The Spirit you received does not make you slaves, so that you live in fear again; rather, the Spirit you received brought about your adoption to sonship. And by him we cry, "Abba, Father."

ROMANS 8:15 NIV

She hurt you in ways that no child should be hurt. You still carry the scars of both the abuse and the ugly words. The grief almost buried you alive. It's taken years to seek help and find healing. Now she's gone. She's passed away, no longer free to torment you or stir up animosity. You're facing a perplexing mixture of emotions—relief, anger, guilt. . .you name it. How can you begin to reconcile those feelings after all you've been through? And how do you go about offering forgiveness to someone who's not even here anymore, someone who never thought she needed to be forgiven in the first place? Let Me start by showing you the unconditional love and care that a real parent should have shown. After that, take your broken heart—picture holding it in your hands—and give it to Me. I will treat it with great care and will breathe new life into it. I will show you how to forgive. It will be a process, but if you stick with Me, you'll be able to release that abuser once and for all. She will no longer have the ability to haunt (or taunt) you. Every emotional bond to your abuser will be broken in My name. We have some deep work to do, but it will be worth it. . .I promise. Freedom beckons. Take My hand.

Pre-Grief

Then his servants said to him, "What is this thing that you have done? While the child was alive, you fasted and wept; but when the child died, you arose and ate food." He said, "While the child was still alive, I fasted and wept; for I said, 'Who knows, the LORD may be gracious to me, that the child may live.' But now he has died; why should I fast? Can I bring him back again? I will go to him, but he will not return to me."

2 Samuel 12:21–23 NASB

Your loved one only has a few weeks—or possibly a few days—left. And even though he's right here, even though you're able to still share a few sweet words or a hand squeeze, you sense the inevitable. You're already grieving, and you haven't even lost this precious person yet. Will things get better when the inevitable moment arrives, or will you suffocate in the grief? Dear one, I need you to know that I am as close as your next heartbeat. I'm here, watching the pain on your face, listening to your cries in the night, covering you with My wings as you traverse this awkward and painful road. Letting go isn't easy. Releasing someone into My hands is one of the hardest things you'll ever have to do. But I haven't forgotten you, nor will I leave you hopeless. Take a deep breath. You can lean on Me. We'll get through this together.

THE LOST YEARS

"*I will repay you for the years the locusts have eaten—the great locust and the young locust, the other locusts and the locust swarm— my great army that I sent among you.*"

JOEL 2:25 NIV

Those rebellious years seemed fun in the moment, didn't they? You were the life of the party, careless and free. Or so you thought. Those days eventually caught up with you, and the effects of that careless living are taking their toll, both in your relationships and your physical body. What looked like freedom in the moment turned out to be bondage. Now you're grieving those lost years. They could have been spent with Me. They should have been productive, joyous and brimming with healthy, happy relationships. Instead, they're buried in the abyss, and finding redemptive moments is tough. Let Me challenge you to look forward, not backward. You have plenty of great years ahead. I'll make something beautiful out of these years. They will be golden, because they will be spent with Me. Don't grieve yesterday. Live for today. Set your sights on tomorrow. Your life—the good, the bad, and the ugly—will be a testimony that will lead others to Me. (See what a good, redemptive God I am?)

LOSS OF HOBBIES AND ACTIVITIES

. . . .

Owe no one anything, except to love each other,
for the one who loves another
has fulfilled the law.

ROMANS 13:8 ESV

Oh, how you love to stay active. You've always been on the go: movies, plays, sporting events, concerts. You've enjoyed outdoor activities as well: camping trips, white-water rafting, and all sorts of other adventures. It's been fun to keep the kiddos active, too, offering them dance lessons, gymnastics, and trips to the children's museum. But now your financial situation is different. There's no money for the things you love. You're grieving the loss of these fun experiences and wish you could turn back the hands of time. I understand how difficult financial loss can be, but those dwindling finances don't have to put an end to the activities. With My help, you can come up with creative and enjoyable things to do—as a family, as an individual, and with your peers. Invite your friends over for movie night at home. Make popcorn. Drink hot chocolate. Take your kids on hiking adventures in your neighborhood or a nearby park. Hit the trails on your bike. Follow the local paper to discover free activities in your area. If you really take the time to research, you'll find enough to keep you busy. Most of all, make your activities about relationships, not about the activity itself. See every opportunity to be together as an adventure in itself. I'll teach you a lot during this season. Watch and see.

PTSD: A Complicated Grief

From the end of the earth I call to You when my heart is faint; lead me to the rock that is higher than I. For You have been a refuge for me, a tower of strength against the enemy.

PSALM 61:2–3 NASB

Your loved one is struggling with PTSD (post-traumatic stress disorder). It's been hard to watch and even harder to navigate the relationship. You want to help, not hurt, the situation, but the irritability, accusations, difficulty functioning. . .it's all hard to watch. Emotional outbursts seem to rule the day. How do you adapt to this new normal? The person you knew and loved was never like this. Before. It's like you're dealing with a whole new person, like the happy one died and the sad/bitter one has taken his place. Your grief feels complicated: Which of the two do you mourn? Remember, this is a person in deep pain. He hasn't been able to shake the nightmares, the trauma, or the horror of the situation that shook him to his core. It's time for concentrated prayer, precious girl. Don't give up on him. Guard yourself from outbursts. Make sure you're safe. But don't stop praying. I still love him as much as ever and want to bring peace out of the chaos in his heart and mind. I can do it. If he opens himself up to it, I *will* do it, and you can play a role in his healing if you keep those prayers coming.

TODAY IS A GIFT

. . . .

*"Therefore do not worry about tomorrow,
for tomorrow will worry about itself.
Each day has enough trouble of its own."*

MATTHEW 6:34 NIV

One of the problems with grief is that it robs you of today and forces your gaze backward, to yesterday. It also keeps you from looking ahead to tomorrow. So no matter how bright the future might be, you're unable to see it through the haze. My goal for you is to bring clarity so that you can enjoy today. It's My gift to you. Look at those right in front of you—your friends, your loved ones. They want to spend time with you, to enjoy your presence. I want that as well. I don't want to see you hung up in the past. There's nothing that can be changed there. I don't want you fretting about the things that are coming. I'm already there, ready to walk you through the good and the bad. I want you to focus on right here, right now. Let's lift that veil of grief so you can unwrap the gift that is today.

Praise Your Way Through

. . . .

When he had consulted with the people, he appointed those who sang to the LORD and those who praised Him in holy attire, as they went out before the army and said, "Give thanks to the LORD, for His lovingkindness is everlasting." When they began singing and praising, the LORD set ambushes against the sons of Ammon, Moab and Mount Seir, who had come against Judah; so they were routed.

2 Chronicles 20:21–22 nasb

There's a wonderful story in My Word about a man named Jehoshaphat. He was facing a mighty army, one far too big (and too well armed) to conquer. So Jehoshaphat followed My instruction and sent his worshippers (the Levites) into the battle first. The rest of the army followed behind the worshippers. Despite being outnumbered, the battle was easily won. This story provides a fine example of how I want you to live. If you're facing an enemy (spiritual or physical), the only way to win the battle is to praise your way through it. Like Jehoshaphat, you can start to worship even before the battle begins. In fact, your chances of success increase tremendously when you start the process with praise. I know, I know, you're going through times of grief and pain. You don't feel like praising. This is when it's most important. So lift your head. Lift your voice. We've got a battle to win!

A CHANGE OF VIEW

But we all, with unveiled face, beholding as in a mirror the glory of the Lord, are being transformed into the same image from glory to glory, just as from the Lord, the Spirit.

2 CORINTHIANS 3:18 NASB

Your perspective has changed. Your worldview has shifted. The people you used to hang with were like minded, but you no longer agree with their philosophies or their approach to life. I've watched as you've gone through a radical transformation, one instigated by My Spirit. Your heart is now beating in sync with Mine, and this thrills Me. But now you have a situation that needs to be dealt with. Your old crowd is a symbol of all you used to be, not all you could be. So, as much as it hurts, I need you to take a few steps away from those who would hold you back. I know this idea grieves you. I'm not asking you to give up on the friendships, just to focus on relationships that will help you grow in Me. This change in perspective will take you to brand-new places, and I will lead every step of the way. I've got amazing things in store. That's why I need your complete focus. No turning back, My child. No turning back.

LOSS OF POTENTIAL

For we are His workmanship, created in Christ Jesus for good works, which God prepared beforehand so that we would walk in them.

EPHESIANS 2:10 NASB

Potential. It's a word you've used many times, both in your own journey and the journeys of your children or loved ones. In many ways, potential is like a dream, one you hope to see fulfilled. But I've been watching as many of the people you adore have frittered away their potential. Their poor choices have left you scratching your head. I've been saddened by their decisions, too. I placed inside of every person the potential to accomplish much for My kingdom's sake. It's heartbreaking to see so many turn and go their own way. Oh, but I'm so proud of you! You don't just have potential; you've already accomplished much. With My help, you've touched the lives of many. And you have quite the road ahead of you. Because of your great, God-given potential, you have the ability to develop into something—someone—extraordinary. The days ahead are bright. I'm already excited just thinking about it!

Unresolved Grief

In peace I will both lie down and sleep,
for You alone, O LORD,
make me to dwell in safety.

PSALM 4:8 NASB

You're all cried out. There are no more tears. You're completely empty, hollow. All that's left is the sting of what used to be. Getting out of bed is a chore. The grief is beginning to affect your physical health and your ability to perform everyday tasks. I see how this is zapping you and want to make sure you're aware that I'm here to help. I know it seems impossible in the middle of the battle, but I truly can show you how to resolve what you're feeling. It's going to take time, but this will be one of the most critical decisions of your life. If you leave these feelings unresolved, it could eventually wreak havoc in your life. I don't want to see you grow physically ill because you were unable to let go. So let Me help you. Let Me guide you. There will be an ultimate resolution when you place things in My hands. I don't do things halfway. I'll take you all the way through from grief to comfort, and I'll show you how to take every step along the way.

MENOPAUSE

Therefore I urge you, brethren, by the mercies of God, to present your bodies a living and holy sacrifice, acceptable to God, which is your spiritual service of worship. And do not be conformed to this world, but be transformed by the renewing of your mind, so that you may prove what the will of God is, that which is good and acceptable and perfect.

ROMANS 12:1–2 NASB

You're going through "the change." That's what your mother called it, anyway. I created your body to morph as you age, so Mama was right. But I can see you're perplexed by the many shifts in your body, internally and externally. You're not exactly thrilled with all that's happening. In fact, a glance in the mirror makes you cringe. And every time you think about the word *menopause*, you get a little teary. The days of childbearing are behind you now. Why does that grieve you so? It's not as if you had planned for more children. Still, the knowledge that you can never get pregnant again has you feeling reminiscent and sad. The idea that you're shifting from one stage of life to another is sobering, but I want to remind you that this next season is going to be amazing. You'll be moving into many more years, free from monthly woes. And even though there will be some adjustments, I'll see you through.

GRIEVING A FRIEND'S LOSS

. . . .

*When Job's three friends, Eliphaz the Temanite,
Bildad the Shuhite and Zophar the Naamathite,
heard about all the troubles that had come upon
him, they set out from their homes and met
together by agreement to go and sympathize
with him and comfort him.*

JOB 2:11 NIV

It's so hard to watch your good friend struggle, but never more so than now. This recent loss has completely devastated her. I see how brokenhearted she is, and you're feeling the weight of her grief, too. You're wishing you could do something to make this better for her. But what? First of all, let her know that you love her. And let her know that you care deeply about all that she's lost. She will feel My love as you wrap your arms around her and offer encouraging words. She doesn't need platitudes. This is no time for fake cheer. This precious friend needs a shoulder. I'm whispering sweet words into her ears, even now, but she needs to hear from you, too. So bake that cake. Pick up a couple of cups of good coffee. Then head to her place, ready to spend some time holding her hand and listening to her heart.

NEVER SEPARATED

· ·

Neither height nor depth, nor anything else in all creation, will be able to separate us from the love of God that is in Christ Jesus our Lord.

ROMANS 8:39 NIV

Remember how you played hide-and-seek as a child? There was a wild excitement in your heart as you hid from others. You prayed you wouldn't be found. Sometimes your life has felt a bit like a game of hide-and-seek, hasn't it? I've watched as you've pulled away from your brothers and sisters in the Lord. Like the childhood game, you haven't wanted to be found. Life would be easier if everyone just left you alone. Oh, but I will never do that. I want to remind you, once again, that I'm right there in that closet with you. When you're hiding under the covers, I'm as close as your next breath. And though you try valiantly to escape My glance, it's impossible. I'll never leave you, no matter where you hide. If you go to the highest mountain, I'll find you. If you plummet to the depths, I'll be there. If you give yourself over to grief, hiding away in plain sight, I will find you and rescue you. That's how much I adore you. So no hide-and-seek with Me. Let's draw close instead.

This Fallen World

"For God so loved the world, that He gave His only begotten Son, that whoever believes in Him shall not perish, but have eternal life."

JOHN 3:16 NASB

You've grieved many things in your life—losses so great that you hardly knew how to pick up the pieces and go on. And yet you're here, healed and whole. Today I want to talk with you about something that matters greatly to Me: grieving the lost. Do you have a heart for those around you who don't know Me? Have you shared the Gospel with them? All around the globe there are people hungry for Me. They don't even realize what they're searching for, but deep in their souls they are longing for a relationship with their Creator. Many are looking at believers like you and see that you have survived life's greatest catastrophes. They want to know your secret. Will you share it? Do you have the courage? I will use you as a witness if you'll let Me. Don't be afraid. I'll open the right doors. I'll give you the courage to speak. Most of all, I'll give you a heart for the lost so that your passion, your heart, your thoughts are for them. With My perspective and My courage, you will do great and mighty things for the kingdom.

Beauty for Ashes

. . . .

The LORD has anointed me to proclaim good
news to the poor. He has sent me to bind up
the brokenhearted, to proclaim freedom for the
captives. . .to proclaim the year of the LORD's
favor and the day of vengeance of our God,
to comfort all who mourn, and provide for those
who grieve in Zion—to bestow on them a crown of
beauty instead of ashes, the oil of joy instead
of mourning, and a garment of praise instead
of a spirit of despair. They will be called
oaks of righteousness, a planting of the
LORD for the display of his splendor.

ISAIAH 61:1–3 NIV

Do you see, child? Does it all make sense now? I will always give you beauty in place of ashes. No matter how dismal your situation, no matter how deep the grief, I can (and will) make your life a thing of beauty. I long to give you the oil (salve) of joy. Why? To replace your mourning. I've even got a special garment picked out, just for you. When you slip it over your head, praises begin to rise. More than anything I want you to know that you are on display— yes, even now, after all you've been through—an oak of righteousness. I'm proud of you. Your journey has been hard, but you make Me want to square My shoulders and say, "That's My girl, My beautiful, holy girl."

GUILT OVER ENJOYING LIFE AGAIN

I believe that I shall look upon the goodness of the LORD in the land of the living!

PSALM 27:13 ESV

It doesn't make sense. Not long ago you were grieving the loss of someone you cared deeply for. Now you're feeling more hopeful. You've rejoined the land of the living and are enjoying life once more. This is exactly what I planned, and it thrills My heart to see that you're ready to make a fresh start. But I see that you're feeling guilty over this newfound freedom from grief. How can you revert back to a normal life after losing someone so special? Shouldn't you grieve longer? Harder? Are others wondering why you aren't curled up in a ball crying? My child, I've longed for this moment when the tentacles of grief would loosen and you would be free to run, to skip, to play. I've longed to see that smile on your face and to watch you communicate with others. I adore that laugh of yours. It's been far too long since I've heard it. So don't grieve the lack of grief. Celebrate the fact that I've done a work in your heart, and trust that I have amazing days ahead.

From Mourning to Dancing

. . . .

You turned my wailing into dancing;
you removed my sackcloth and clothed me with joy.

PSALM 30:11 NIV

❧

You're My child and I love you. Let Me say that again: you're My child and I love you! It's been a journey so far, this life you've lived. And though you've had some discouraging times, much of the road has been filled with blissful moments. There are plenty of great days ahead, dear one. Don't ever let the past define you. Don't ever let your grief keep you knotted up. I need you free to soar, free to dance. All those hardships you've faced? Think of them as choreographed steps in the great dance of life, one we have shared every step of the way. Our dance wouldn't be the same if you hadn't gone through those rough patches. Oh, but what a lovely dance it's been thus far! Filled with ups and downs, ins and outs. Our choreography is graceful and garnished with beautiful moments. My favorite part? The lifts. How exquisite, to witness the many times I've lifted you above your circumstances then set you back on solid footing once more. How precious, those moments when I've held you close so you could hear My heartbeat. We make a good couple, you and I. So I'm going to extend My hand today and again tomorrow. In fact, I'm asking you to be a partner for all the days of your life. The music is starting. Won't you join Me in the dance?

SUBJECT INDEX